Sacred Chaos

Marie-Louise von Franz, Honorary Patron

**Studies in Jungian Psychology
by Jungian Analysts**

Daryl Sharp, General Editor

SACRED CHAOS

Reflections on God's Shadow
and the Dark Self

Françoise O'Kane

The original manuscript of this book was published in French by Georg Editeur SA, Geneva, 1990. A limited edition in English, translated by the author, was made available under the title *God's Shadow and the Novice's Stones: A Reflection on the Dark Self* (published by Albatross Books, Mönchaltorf, Switzerland, 1991).

Sacred Chaos is a revision by the author of *God's Shadow and the Novice's Stones,* edited by Inner City Books.

Canadian Cataloguing in Publication Data

O'Kane, Françoise
    Sacred chaos: reflections on God's shadow and the dark Self

(Studies in Jungian psychology by Jungian analysts; 64)

Includes bibliographical references and index.

ISBN 0-919123-65-1

1. Shadow (Psychoanalysis).
2. Good and evil—Psychological aspects.
3. Theodicy. 4. Jung, C.G. (Carl Gustav), 1875-1961.
I. Title. II. Series.

BF175.5.S55053 1994   150.19'5   C94-931020-4

INNER CITY BOOKS
Box 1271, Station Q, Toronto, Canada M4T 2P4
Telephone (416) 927-0355
FAX (416) 924-1814

Honorary Patron: Marie-Louise von Franz.
Publisher and General Editor: Daryl Sharp.
Senior Editor: Victoria Cowan.

INNER CITY BOOKS was founded in 1980 to promote the understanding and practical application of the work of C.G. Jung.

Cover: Wooden sculpture of a devil, in the village square of Bessans, Savoie, France. (Photo courtesy Michael J. O'Kane.)

Index by Daryl Sharp

Printed and bound in Canada by
University of Toronto Press Incorporated

Contents

See final pages for descriptions of other Inner City Books

Foreword

The notion of shadow is central to analytical psychology. It is both a theoretical concept and a powerful visual image. What Jung means when he writes of the shadow could be expressed by an analogy with the terrestrial globe, one half of which is illuminated by the sun. As the earth rotates, its different continents are alternately in the light or in the shadow. Night always reigns over one half of the globe. Transferring this image to the individual level, we may say that part of our being is in the light: we are conscious of certain personal traits that we consider positive. We may use these qualities to adapt to the world, and so they are valuable.

The dark side of personality remains invisible and unconscious; it is perceived as negative and poorly adapted. Its qualities may be a hindrance to adaptation and the individual may think them useless. Hence there is a tendency for people to negate their shadow and to repress it.

However, just as the earth rotates on its own axis, during the course of an individual's life the other side of the personality starts emerging. We are then forced to acknowledge qualities we had denied and to discover their value. Generally speaking, this change happens when we enter the second half of life. This is never an easy passage and it provokes all sorts of resistances. Confronting these may be seen as the hard daily bread we all must chew.

It is relatively easy to accept the above image as it applies to the shadow of our ego. Yet, Françoise O'Kane is writing about the *shadow of God*. We have learned to see God as a personification of absolute Good or Love; is it at all possible that He has a shadow? Can God personify Evil and want our perdition? The author leads us to the Garden of Gethsemane where these questions are given an affirmative—and somewhat extraordinary—answer.

In everyday therapeutic work, analysts may hold to particular theories. Crises in adolescence and marriage are usually resolved, sooner or later. In such cases, the process aims at dealing with certain symptoms and not so much at reaching to a deeper level, although in a way it always will. Once the crisis is over, one may be pleased about the "progress" and go back to "normal" life. But sometimes the analyst is confronted with those whose suffering is truly unfathomable and who are really lost in God's shadow, in a dark night where time stands still. In these cases, analysts need to find an attitude that will allow them to endure within a darkness from which it seems every hope has been excluded. Here, talking about progress makes absolutely no sense.

Françoise O'Kane goes beyond simple optimism. She shows that an answer to the ultimate despair is given by the psyche and that it is possible, *Deo concedente,* to discover it.

At a time when our highest values, virtues and abilities are turning against us, the whole of humanity risks finding itself in God's shadow. Thus it is worth listening to her message, for answers to global problems must always be found by individuals; and, as analysts, we must care for the individual.

C.T. Frey-Wehrlin
Zürich

Preface

In some Eskimo tribes living around Hudson Bay, novice shamans undergo an apprenticeship with an experienced master. The most important stage of the apprenticeship, the actual making of the shaman, takes place when they spend weeks or months isolated from the group in a desolate place, without food. They patiently rub stones until they reach the stage of "illumination," during which, after being reduced to their own skeleton and having learned the ritual name of each of their bones, they get to know their "life soul." (The Igluliks have two souls, a name soul and a life soul, with only the latter being eternal.)

This image accompanied and comforted me as I wrote about the confrontation with the dark Self. It was neither the shaman nor the healer who felt important but rather the slow rubbing of mineral against mineral, a monotonous noise which seemed to find an echo in the eternal. God's shadow, the dark Self which the Eskimo novice meets on his journey, provokes unspeakable suffering in individuals whose life it overshadows. It is connected to death, destruction and madness. But, paradoxically, it is also connected to vitality. Its power is as great as that of the life force in us. Light and positive values are better accepted by society and often by the analyst. Can we accept that God has a shadow and that He therefore does not simply love us? Or even that love and hate are indissoluble components of our relationship to Him?

This book was written by many different people. It is still in process, with me and with others. We are on a long journey, lost in a cosmos ruled by both loving and destructive powers. We can only travel along those paths where our hearts rather than theories take us. The original French version was written at a point when I hoped that putting into words questions and fragments of answers might help me perceive better what was happening in and around me. I felt like a traveler attempting to draw a map by looking at fragments of landscape carried in memory. Much has happened since then, but the map still consists only of moments and patterns. I have reformulated some passages, to put clearer words around particular ideas and feelings, but no more.

As I was translating my original French manuscript, I noticed that I had often written about what should not be done, as if my chief intention were to be critical. I believe that this happened—and had to happen—for dialectical reasons. Only by contrasting two diametrically opposed approaches could I hope to see a bit more clearly where I was going. Also, positive values are so dominant, in and outside analysis, that, when talking about the negative, one inevitably feels one has to shout in order to be heard. But I am not a pessimist; on the contrary, I know that healing does take place. Further, by painting a rather somber picture of the confrontation with the Self and its dark side, I found a peace which carries far greater value than arguments for or against any specific orientation.

Of the people who traveled with me, many must remain anonymous, be they friends or analysands. But a few who contributed more directly to the evolution of this book must be mentioned.

C.T. Frey-Wehrlin supported my natural taste for paradox. Paul Brutsche gave me the trust to carry on writing. Michael O'Kane and John Peck read a first draft of the English manuscript; their suggestions greatly improved the text, which has also benefited from the delicate editing touch of Daryl Sharp and Victoria Cowan.

The comments brought by Kaj Noschis and by a number of students to the seminars I gave at the C.G. Jung Institute in Zürich further helped me clarify my ideas. Some of their reactions showed me clearly that analytical psychology urgently needs to find means of accepting and integrating the dark Self. To all of them, thank you.

Part One

"The Universe is the Mirror of the People,"
the old Teachers tell us, "and each
person is a Mirror to every other person."
Any idea, person or object can be a
Medicine Wheel, a Mirror, for man.

—Hyemeyohsts Storm, *Song of Heyoehkah.*

1
The Unfathomable

This book's point of departure is the duality inherent in the Self archetype. In Jung's theoretical concept, the Self contains both light and shadow aspects which coexist, are irreducible and do not derive from each other. They are not endowed with a value per se: the formulation of a hierarchical system in which good would be better than evil is the ego's doing.

My intention is not to discuss Jung's thinking at a theoretical level. However, his ideas serve as the backdrop to the questions I ask, and they will be used to support the conclusions I draw. It is well known that, over the years, Jung modified his approach and that his theory was subject to a continuous process of transformation. Here I am satisfied with a very basic definition of the Self as light and shadow, illness and health, life and death, with all of these fundamentally given. My inquiries are oriented toward a potential relationship with this entity and, particularly, with its dark, irrational, unfathomable and threatening aspects.

The irrational and the dark are inherent to the psyche; they may be repressed, at a cost, but they cannot be eliminated. What is more, it seems that every analyst has seen one or more cases in which, as far back as childhood, the psyche has been dominated by the dark aspects of the Self, sometimes—often?—without apparent reason. In other cases, it is possible to find a cause to this constellation, by ascertaining concrete roots in the family background or in specific events. But one may wonder whether these explanations are sufficient. Indeed, further inquiry frequently reveals a paradoxical therapeutic experience. A few individuals, whom one would expect to have suffered more than others from their family constellation or from a traumatic childhood, seem to have escaped this fate, while others are faced with very serious psychic trouble, despite their family background not being particularly problematic.

We may also think of the paradox presented by cases in which, at least during long intervals, the unconscious produces only shadow motifs and is unable to suggest any positive development. The concept of compensation may be used to explain what is happening when the analysand consciously adopts an attitude unilaterally oriented toward light. But what about the patients who find themselves in a deep depression and whose dreams are just as negative and destructive as their conscious feelings?[1] What about those who appear to have lost all contact with their unconscious roots or, even, have almost totally repressed them because, in their experience, the Self can only overwhelm, threaten or destroy? In such cases it is not so easy to find an explanation.

It would, of course, be possible to trace further in the genealogies of these analysands a difficult psychic inheritance which may have bypassed one or more generations. In the specific case of an endogenous depression, one should also take into account the physiological inheritance. But does this suffice? I do not believe that every symptom can be explained in terms of cause and effect. What is more, causal statements are certainly no great comfort to patients caught in immovable suffering.

Further, we may wonder about the numerous questions still connected to the notion of mental disease, and particularly to the etiology of schizophrenia. What do we know about psychosis? We treat endogenous psychoses, we are able to relieve certain forms of depression, and medication may free schizophrenics from some of their symptoms. These achievements do not imply that we really understand the mechanisms involved. And, even if clear causes could be defined, this would not necessarily mean a cure is possible. What is a "cure" in this context? Medical doctors cure diseases, but the analyst's role is that of helping the analysand find "healing"—a better relationship to life—rather than a cure in terms of eradicating symptoms.

To my mind, the central question must be whether and how analytical psychology may bring about healing. It is not sufficient to consider neurosis or psychosis as failings or diseases, with all the negative connotations such formulations carry. The role played by the shadow aspects of the Self in relation to mental illness must be investigated. And, last but not least, we must try to understand what place the shadow aspects of the Self occupy in relation to psychic health.

Beyond the numerous questions connected to concrete phenomena and the analysand's experience, a far more fundamental debate must be opened: that of individual destiny. Why is it that one person rather than another is compelled to experience nefarious, destructive and frightening aspects of being? What is the meaning, or is there any, to this constella-

---

[1] I use the terms analysand, client and patient alternately, in order to avoid too many repetitions of the word analysand; but, in general, I have reserved the term patient for those suffering from relatively severe psychic problems.

tion? How can such people accept their fate? Is it enough, or even possible, to try to help them connect with the other pole, with life and creation?

Of course, mental disease represents an extreme case. The majority of people who go into analysis suffer from a neurosis. We tend to try to help on the basis of a hypothesis according to which their specific biography must be "treated," rewritten, reexperienced, in order both to eliminate those elements that are causing difficulties and to make their life richer. But there may be too much of a tendency to explain everything, to treat every symptom, to correct any deviance.

Developmental theories in particular provide therapists with a comforting framework. Broadly speaking, they offer models of an ideal development; once the elements that the patient lacked in childhood and the ensuing personal problems have been defined, the therapist is able to approach the work on a relatively clear—safe?—basis. But, for instance, those symptoms and reactions described as characteristic of a narcissistic personality can also be viewed from a different perspective: they are part of an attempt at survival, a way for the individual to confront despair over a life that, for whatever reason, has been dominated by shadow and destruction. At this level, questions of a very different order must be asked, more directly related to existential aspects.

Obviously, theories of all kinds are useful. But, once we have decided—depending on the theory chosen—that a certain individual suffers from an incomplete or unstable personality, for instance that the ego-Self axis has been insufficiently developed (Erich Neumann) or that the family background was not able to provide a stable enough self (Hans Kohut),[2] how do we enter into the case? How do we work with the client?

My intention is not to review possible approaches. But, to my mind, there is a gap between theory and practice. The preference given to a specific theoretical model greatly influences the transference-countertransference relationship. But this relationship is extremely complex and cannot be explained by theory only. Further, the theory should be reserved for outside the sessions, as a means of understanding a case on a broader basis, while direct therapeutic interaction rests on a more irrational, more emotional basis. And, again, we may wonder what role the dark Self plays.

Another aspect interests me: regardless of the therapeutic theory or

---

[2] In Jungian terminology, Kohut's self would be called ego. Jung himself in his later writings did not capitalize self when referring to it as an archetype, but here I use Self throughout in order to differentiate it from the mundane ego-self.

method, we, as analysts or as therapists, tend to focus on a more global approach that assumes the individual suffers from a "lack," that something went wrong, and that a positive evolution, including an improvement or a correction of this situation should be our goal. We may then hope for or even promise a transformation far too quickly. The notion of transformation itself may stem more from the analyst's fantasies than from the true nature of the psyche. Does the client's personality eventually become so different from what it was before the analysis?

One may object that, things being as they are, the analysand is there precisely because of a lack, because he or she has problems. Obviously, the analysand's hope is a powerful antidote to despair; it always plays a central role in the analytic process. It is not this that I am questioning. My criticism concerns the preconceived idea that the individual's suffering may be alleviated only through a correction, an elimination of the "original fault," or even through a radical transformation.

At this level, healing would involve restructuring the personality according to an ideal model, or correcting missed developments, so as to lead the individual back to the norms inherent to what we—society—consider to be positive. It would also involve, probably, a real transformation, but would it be for the better? I have seen analysands who were very dedicated to finding their way, but who were following quite an abstract model, striving for the perfection of the hero who overcomes all the darkest aspects of life. They were thus enslaved to an unreachable ideal, under which they suffered greatly. If such clients are to become free, the analytic process must work toward helping them renounce this model instead of (implicitly) supporting it. I am criticizing, therefore, a professional bias toward ideas of improvement, progress and light—or even enlightenment—and I am wondering whether, because of this bias, the analyst's work is not in the process of being appropriated by society and influenced by growth models that attribute highest priority to technical progress.

Jung, on the other hand, sees the psyche as endowed with a capacity to heal itself, to find spontaneously (that is, as long as the ego does not interfere) a balance in which the unilateral attitude of the conscious standpoint is compensated and broadened, so that neurosis (or worse) is avoided. According to him, the Self guides—and sometimes imposes—this process; as the "objective" psyche, the unconscious knows what is right for the individual. The basis of genuine healing would be established when the ego, having found the "propitious attitude" toward the messages from the unconscious, is in contact with those elements of the Self that are able to correct and complete the conscious attitude.[3] These ideas also underly the notion of the process of individuation—a concept which, in itself, may be subjected to a critical discussion, if only because it has too often been understood as implying a linear growth.

But, here, the interesting questions stem from the duality of the Self in relation to the dialectical process taking place within the whole psyche. What will be the place occupied by the dark elements? How can an entity bring healing if, within it, light and shadow, good and evil, life and death, and, depending on the case, even health and illness or psychic health and madness, are closely interrelated? And what is "healing"? Does it exist? Is it a triumph of health?

And, more than anything else, how can we justify the approach according to which we consider certain individuals to be sick—or neurotic, or psychotic, or whatever diagnosis—and mark an artificial demarcation line separating the chosen from the damned? What happened to our own shadow, to the dark aspects in ourselves? What gives us the right, when we say that we are able to "heal," to imply that we are standing on one side only—the right one—of this line?

A fundamental problem, related to the choice of a terminology, now becomes apparent: a number of the terms used here so far contain a value judgment, since they express dichotomies resting on a basic contrast between positive and negative. In fact, the ego designates anything that it does not like as negative, whereas the Self simply *is* as it is, and unites the opposites without considering them more or less valuable. In the Self, values do not exist per se and, ideally, a descriptive terminology should not imply them. But it is quite impossible to avoid attributing values when using language.[4] Therefore, I must stress again that, since my intention is basically to question the pertinence of these values, great caution should

---

[3] By propitious (rather than right) I mean the best possible attitude at a purely pragmatic level, in a sense not too far from that expressed by Jung when he wrote that "the only way to get at them [unconscious contents] in practice is to try to attain a conscious attitude which allows the unconscious to co-operate instead of being driven into opposition." ("The Psychology of the Transference," *The Practice of Psychotherapy,* CW 16, par. 366) [CW refers throughout to *The Collected Works of C.G. Jung]*

[4] In "Das Eisige Selbst—ein Versuch" [The Icy Self—an Essay], Enrico Francot uses the contrast warm/cold in order to designate the two poles of the Self. This is an excellent idea.

be applied. The contrasts above come spontaneously to mind and they are used in a purely tentative manner. They should not be understood as attributing an intrinsic value to either the Self or its components. Nor should these contrasting pairs be understood as necessarily coinciding. For example, the pair light/shadow does not correspond to a contrast between conscious and unconscious, and even less to that between life and death (the unconscious being as much connected to life as is the conscious). But scrupulous differentiation would involve unnecessary complexity and I shall often simplify.

Another problem is that the English expression "the dark Self" encompasses a whole scale of meanings. Dark in this sense implies simultaneously the dimensions of overshadowed, sinister or even destructive. It also contains an element of mystery, of ambiguity, of the unknown or even of the secret. I shall sometimes specify the relevant aspect and sometimes stay with the more global word "dark." I am actually more interested in the overshadowed and mysterious aspects of the Self than in the contrast between good and evil, because this contrast is clearly connected with a moral evaluation.

One dimension must be defined more precisely: shadow. I have chosen to place my reflections at a relatively general level, that of the Self; when I use the term shadow it is thus in a very broad sense, broader than that intended by Jung when he writes of the personal or collective shadow. By shadow I mean the dark, nefarious aspects inherent in the Self. These will of course manifest both at a personal and at a collective level, but they also have a much more impersonal, archetypal quality than is generally meant by the term shadow in a Jungian sense. At that level, the negative pole of the Self does not correspond exactly to the negative pole of the ego (the negative aspect of the personal or collective shadow *strictu senso*). In everyday practice, this archetypal shadow may manifest in series of negative synchronicities, in concrete diseases, in blockages, but also quite often simply in deep depression and a feeling of absolute hopelessness. The analysand becomes stuck in darkness and, through the transference-countertransference, the analyst too may suffer despair.

It would be possible to make other theoretical distinctions or to outline more clearly the elements involved in the dark Self. One could, for instance, formulate this in terms of further archetypes or complexes ("the negative mother" among others), or situate the influence of the dark Self with respect to the development of the ego-Self axis. Or one could try to elaborate on the relationship between dark and light aspects of the Self and the archetypal stages Jung describes when he writes about the individuation process (integration of shadow, anima/animus, etc.). I believe that Jung, when he formulated his terminology, established descriptive categories that, on the surface at least, help grasp better the reality of the psyche; but this reality—in particular the Self—still constitutes a mysterious "other" that remains unfathomable. The terminology offers a structure and clarifies certain points. It risks providing the illusion of a better knowledge. But it cannot eliminate the fundamentally paradoxical and unknowable dimensions of this "something" which has been called the Self.

As psychic reality can only be grasped through a nonrational awareness, it seems better to accept a relatively global approach, at which the unexplained and the mysterious may, by interacting with better known elements, contribute to further discoveries—even if this happens at the cost of not using a very precise terminology and not always developing every implication of the ideas presented.

After this digression, I want to come back to my original question. It seems legitimate to wonder if the notion that the psyche may heal itself necessarily implies that the positive, the light or even life must win. The term "healing" contains in itself an evaluation, the idea of improvement. But is this striving for a positive evolution always justified? Are we not falling into the trap of wanting to formulate a progressive model? In many cases, in fact, healing consists in a search, together with the analysand, for means to accept an overshadowed personal destiny, and to render fruitful its negative dimensions. Health is always an equilibrium in which equal parts are attributed to illness, despair and suffering.[5]

It is because I am attempting to clarify the elements inherent in the notion of "healing" that I am asking these questions and not because I reject the possibility that it may take place. Jung's psychology implies an optimistic view of man and life, or rather a viewpoint in which the confrontation with the Self may come to a happy—not merry, but fortunate or just—ending. To my mind, our task as analysts is not to help analysands enjoy the proper functioning our society considers so valuable. And one should not be more optimistic than Jung himself, who was perfectly aware of both the resources and the limits of human nature.

---

[5] See A.J. Ziegler, *Morbismus, von der Besten aller Gesundheiten* [Morbidism, the Best of Health].

Those cases in which, objectively, negative aspects are dominant have been mentioned above. The opposite situation also exists, where the individual identifies with the positive pole; and it may be just as problem-laden—if only because it provokes an activation, in the unconscious, of the negative counterweight. But the ego tends to approve of the positive, and of light. What is positive is healthy, acceptable; what deviates is unhealthy; health is closely connected to the notion of good, while madness is often equated to evil. A whole reflection could be developed on the manner in which different societies define and evaluate these dimensions.

However, although the individual always lives in a society and this dimension should not be forgotten, we are dealing here with a more subjective focus, concerned with the manner in which an individual perceives his or her own being and may find ways of accepting it. At this level, as much as at a more theoretical level concerned with the nature of the Self, one may wonder whether any positive result has been achieved by the attribution of pejorative labels to the dark aspects of experience.

The Jungian model should, at any rate, warn us against such labeling. As we have seen, the two poles of the Self coexist, one contrasting with the other: light/shadow, good/evil, health/illness. Any attempt at favoring one pole will thus, inevitably, bring about an imbalance and disturb a co-existence that is indispensable to life itself. At the beginning of his book on madness, John Weir Perry formulates a colorful image of what may happen when the pole of madness has been eliminated. Although I am concerned not only with phenomena connected to psychosis, I would like to quote two passages that are applicable to other dimensions of the Self:

> Do we have the right any longer to regard this state [schizophrenia] as mere mental disease and disorder? For what, then, would we make of the fact that some people emerge from such an episode "weller than well," as one psychiatrist has put it? That is, some come out of this state with a newly quick-ened capacity for depth in their concerns, their callings, and their relation-ships. What do we make of the fact that, when out of their senses, some people have experiences perhaps of beauty, perhaps of terror, but always with implications of awesome depth, and that when they reemerge out of their craze and into their so-called normal ego, they may shut the trapdoor after them and close out their vision once more and become prosaic in the extreme, straitened in a bland and shallow usualness? What goes wrong when someone becomes a visionary, looking into the heart of his cosmos and of his fellow beings around him, only when he is "sick," only to become blind, constricted, and timid, understanding nothing, when he is "well" again, dependent for the rest of his days perhaps on a drug to keep this soul

and its vision dampened down and safely out of reach?

It does sound as if there may be two opposite kinds of madness: a madness of the left, full of ecstasy and terror and of the bewildering encounter with spiritual and demonic powers in the psyche; and a madness of the right, hollowed out in bland impoverishment and narrowness, in which the conventions and concreteness of the mundane world are taken for self-evident reality.[6]

Perry writes further that we all live "a hair's breadth" away from a state of being in which reality is not perceived in a rational manner, and that we allow that world—that of rites, myths and dreams, of religion and of poetry—to manifest itself only in generally accepted terms. He adds that we all live, all the time, along two axes, which imply two ways of perceiving reality and, thus, two kinds of reality. He defines these two realities by referring to Jung: in the first, the knowledge of the ego is preponderant, with its day-to-day approach to an everyday world; in the second, a deeper knowledge, a suprapersonal wisdom, helps us to grasp what is not yet clear or conscious.[7] Perry then concludes:

> In my opinion the real pathology in psychosis does not reside in the "mental content," the images and the symbolic sequences. All of that appears to be natural psychic process, present and working in all of us. This is normal madness, so to speak. The schizophrenic "disorder" lies rather in the ego, which suffers from a constricted consciousness that has been educated out of its needed contact with the natural elements of the psychic life, both emotion and image. The madness is perhaps required but comes in overwhelming strength. The need of the schizoid personality is to learn to perceive symbolic meanings as they pertain to the living of one's psychic life, and thus to keep connected with the ever-enriching wellsprings of the emotions which nourish that life. The problem of the prepsychotic state is how to discover the impassioned life, and nature has its own answer in the form of a turbulent ordeal, a trial by immersion in the source of the passions—that is a psychosis.[8]

What Perry says about psychosis may be transposed to our discussion. The disease suffered by the neurotic—who, while apparently not functioning too badly, has problems and feels a painful lack of vitality—is provoked by an ego that has not succeeded in finding an adequate relationship to the dark aspects of the Self. We may all suffer from this lack, living as we do in a society where absolute priority is attributed to the positive. In

---

[6] *The Far Side of Madness,* p. 6.

[7] See *Psychology and Alchemy,* CW 12, pars. 342-400 and epilogue.

[8] *Far Side of Madness,* p. 11.

this sense, the discovery of a propitious attitude would be all the more vital for those who are dominated by aspects that have been rejected by society. And, again, the question arises: is it sufficient to give them a drug "to keep this soul and its vision dampened down," that is, to feed them with positive elements or to neutralize the negative ones? Or would the propitious attitude not consist in rediscovering the value of the "bewildering encounter with . . . demonic powers in the psyche," and thereby in reassessing the value of what society considers negative?

As I have said, I do not believe that we can heal by repressing sick or demonic aspects or by compensating them with a kind of absolute normality. On the contrary, we need to accompany the analysand in a search for means of confronting these aspects, of integrating and accepting them in such a way that they will find a place within the totality of the personality and be thus transformed.

At this level, the notion of shadow integration may be confusing. The shadow cannot, by definition, be "integrated" in the sense that it would disappear or become unimportant. Every time one aspect of the shadow is brought to light, another part of the psyche moves into the dark. Whenever a new attitude is adopted, it is at the cost of another potential behavior that becomes part of the shadow. In cases where sinister dimensions have become overwhelming, it is not always possible to constellate enough positive energy to balance the destructive aspects. The healing that could take place would, then, result not so much from an integration in the sense of a shift in shadow elements, but from the depotentiation, through a specific attitude, of the negative energies. In other words, it would not be through an attempt at constellating the positive pole in order to compensate for the negative, but through a modification of the relationship between the ego and the dark pole, that negative energies could be deprived of some of their power. This distinction seems important.

The question of whether the Self, or the psyche as a whole, is able to concretely rely on its positive resources must be asked within a methodological approach that avoids quarrels between schools. Every therapist, and an analyst even more so, chooses the approach best suited to his or her personality and experience. I tend to adopt a perspective that is more pragmatic than theoretical. In other words, instead of looking for causes and explanations, I look for means of coping with specific situations. And if I take an apparently critical stance, mentioning more often what should not be done than what has been done, it is for dialectical reasons. By contrasting (extreme) viewpoints I am hoping to formulate an approach that will be useful in everyday practice. This practice is so complex that a degree of generalization and simplification cannot be avoided. The conclusions reached will, of course, remain relatively broad; they will have to be adapted to the nuances inherent in each specific case.

In that sense, we may take it as a premise that, despite our tendency to believe in the positive forces of the Self, many analysands still have rather few occasions for concretely experiencing its positive energy. At the more global level of the group, and in spite of the value attributed to the good and to a positive attitude, we cannot deny that shadow aspects constitute one of the main problems faced by contemporary societies. I believe that it is precisely the individuals who have to cope with the sinister aspects of their own destiny who can teach us how, by recovering a more instinctive, more complete humanity, we may confront this shadow.

I am well aware that a simple statement concerning the ineluctable nature of the dark may, at first, not bring much comfort to one who is suffering. But we are not of more help if we look for clear, reassuring reasons for a person's pain. It is not too useful to choose a mechanistic perspective in which, since the causes are known, it is relatively easy to suggest remedies and even to promise a cure. Does this mean that the analysand will have to bury the hope of ever feeling better? I have, in fact, already answered this question. One may, of course, wonder whether one is not asking too much of a patient looking for relief from pain when one suggests (if only implicitly) an approach including and accepting suffering and despair. I believe that much depends on the atmosphere and on the spirit in which one formulation or another is chosen, and also on the moment when something is said. Many stages in the work will need to be adapted to the manner in which the analysand's unconscious perceives the problem, and the different steps will have to be grounded in a strong enough transference-countertransference relationship. It is at this level that the vital process is carried. In going together through darkness, analyst and analysand may hope to find meaning, without needing constantly to verbalize the emotional interaction supporting the process.

The analyst's work must be founded in Eros, in all its aspects—including the chthonic and the negative. My own experience has convinced me that, as soon as the transference-countertransference relationship is stable enough to carry an emotional process, it becomes possible and necessary to take account of the dimensions discussed above. I am not suggesting the analyst should say, "That is the way it is and you only need to . . ." or, worse, "Your dreams are saying that all you have to do is suffer." Everything is a question of sensitivity and empathy, also of formulation, and not much needs to be made explicit. On the surface, at least, the analyst addresses the analysand's ego; this conscious center is not necessarily stable, nor does it always have enough flexibility or energy to confront fundamental problems directly. One must certainly take this into account. But the way in which the analyst chooses to perceive the work influences what happens in the sessions. If the analyst defines the task as "curing the analysand," in the sense of striving for improved functioning within norms that do not take sufficient account of the negative pole of the psyche, the analysis will not evolve as it would were the analyst to accept, and help the analysand accept, the dark aspects overshadowing the personality. Another way of putting this is to say that the analyst's task is to help the analysand carry the burden, rather than to relieve it.

This being said, I do not have too many answers to offer, and perhaps should emphasize that it is the analysands with whom I have worked who have often forced me to face these questions. I have not been able to rest in the illusion that I was really capable of understanding their destiny, nor that I could hope with them that an improvement in a traditional sense could be reached. Thus I can only try to work with them at accepting, without judging and without interfering. I can try to help them discover the feeling of vitality to which other people have easier access. I may try to show them the path of an "initiatic surrender,"[9] an apparently totally irrational submission to the dark.

It is in this sense that I shall attempt to define the components of the propitious attitude, an attitude which includes a conviction that the dark pole of the Self is an inherent part of existential vitality. These components represent tools for providing a new balance. To this end, I shall rely on elements from the wisdom of tribal groups and from cultures of a matriarchal type. This reliance does not imply a negative regression. We are so one-sidedly oriented toward Logos-consciousness that only an extreme compensation in the other direction can hope to succeed.

As for the usefulness of this approach, I would like to add that it need not exclude a much more fundamental attitude, one expressed very well by Alan Loy McGinnis:

---

[9] See below, chap. 5.

Good psychotherapists are something like astronomers who spend their lives studying the stars, trying to find out why certain stellar systems behave as they do and why black holes exist. And at the end they are even more in awe of the grandeur of it all.

Although I will never understand my patients fully, my goal is to sit beside them as they search out themselves. The two of us will study the makeup and watch the movements of this personality, seeking to understand. It would be as presumptuous of me to attempt to overhaul that system as for an astronomer to remake the solar system. If I can help patients understand who God made them to be, and then help them to *be* those men and women, it is quite enough.[10]

---

[10] *The Friendship Factor: How To Get Closer to the People You Care For*, p. 13.

2

God's Shadow

This chapter is meant to provide the reader with some theoretical background that may serve further to ground practice. As indicated previously, it is in the personal level that I am interested; I am trying to find a way to help those individuals who are directly confronted with the dark side of God. Suffering and accepting with little hope of psychic transformation, in or outside analysis, may be the burden these people have to carry.

Clearly, their problem is also related to the much broader questions of God's shadow and the process of the transformation of God Jung wrote about in "Answer to Job."[11] Changes at a collective level are brought about by individuals and, in that sense, I do not give up hope that we may discover new ways of confronting global problems. But my task as an analyst is to accompany individuals along their paths, leaving others to grapple with deep theological questions.

Thus the following discussion of Jung's writings on the dualistic nature of the Self is intended simply to put in a broader context my more pragmatic questions: in the work with analysands, what place is to be given to dark aspects and how can these be confronted?

The *Imago Dei*

Jung's awareness of both the potentials and the limits of human nature is particularly clear when he writes about the Self in analogy to the image of Christ, as a symbol of the God inherent in man, and analyzes the evolution of Christian doctrine. Much of his reflection focuses on the dark Self and its repression. Further, he equates the experience of the Self with an experience of the divine, defining it as a religious event in the true sense of the term:

> The self . . . constitutes the most immediate experience of the Divine which it is psychologically possible to imagine.[12]

---

[11] *Psychology and Religion,* CW 11; see also Edward F. Edinger, *Transformation of the God-Image: An Elucidation of Jung's* Answer to Job.

[12] "Transformation Symbolism in the Mass," *Psychology and Religion,* CW 11, par. 396.

In that sense, and whether we like it or not, analogies with existing religious systems spontaneously come to mind and may help understand the psychological confrontation with the Self. We could, of course, take our departure point from the God-image formulated by tribal religions, where nefarious forces or gods are generally considered to exist, both in man and in the threatening aspects of the cosmos and nature. Religion formulates a means of confronting them in order to survive. Indeed, at a psychological level, the Self shares with nature this aspect of being something that is given and not necessarily understandable rationally.

The attitude expressed by religions of an animistic type is not in itself as primitive as we would sometimes like to think—or as Jung often implies. As opposed to Christianity or other major religious systems, these religions might even be closer to the right psychological attitude toward the Self. It is probably not purely a coincidence if, over the past few decades, movements have appeared, in which "civilized" people attempt to find meaning in the practices elaborated by tribal groups, be it shamanistic rituals or ceremonies that seek a contact with nature spirits. This search may occasionally take an inadequate form, because cultural elements cannot be simply transferred to another system. And the practice by Occidentals of tribal rituals is sometimes more the reflection of personal despair than a true quest for the means to confront repressed dimensions. Still, I believe that we have an unfortunate tendency to believe ourselves less "savage" or less "primitive" than the tribes who elaborated their own mythologies and developed their own rites in order to soothe the gods.

The Christian doctrine remains a strong component of our cultural background; its symbols and its mythology influence the way we feel and think, and they are closer to us than those of the medicine-man. Of course, with regard to the Self our interest must remain more psychological than theological. But, even at this level, Jung's analysis of the evolution of the Christian doctrine is useful to a better understanding of potential relations with the Self. Take this passage, for instance:

> Just as we have to remember the gods of antiquity in order to appreciate the psychological value of the anima/animus archetype, so Christ is our nearest analogy of the self and its meaning. . . . Yet, although the attributes of Christ . . . undoubtedly mark him out as an embodiment of the self, looked at from the psychological angle he corresponds to only one half of the archetype. The other half appears in the Antichrist. The latter is just as much a manifestation of the self, except that he consists of its dark aspect. Both are Christian symbols, and they have the same meaning as the image of the

Saviour crucified between two thieves. This great symbol tells us that the progressive development and differentiation of consciousness leads to an ever more menacing awareness of the conflict and involves nothing less than a crucifixion of the ego, its agonizing suspension between irreconcilable opposites. . . . This means, in other words, that in such cases the ego is a suffering bystander who decides nothing but must submit to a decision and surrender unconditionally.[13]

According to the Gnostics, to whom Jung often refers, Christ rejected his own shadow. It is this shadow, the Antichrist, who resides in the unconscious and complements the too one-sided figure of the Redeemer. In other words, Christ was not born without some shadow; but he later attempted to rid himself of this side of his personality. Psychologically speaking, light and shadow are equally important. However, the ego under the influence of religious or moral value judgments is torn by the temptation of identifying either with Christ or with Antichrist. Finally, it can only surrender to forces that are far more powerful than it, or choose not to choose, so as to gain an attitude adapted to the reality of the psyche.

For many centuries, though not originally, Christian doctrine has been dominated by the notion that the ego, as the center of the free individual, may exert a degree of control and choose good over evil. This implies a specific attitude toward the polarity of the divinity; it introduces a dichotomy and attempts to eliminate the evil aspects. Or, rather, it attributes them to the devil, an idea clearly expressed by the Gnostics and by Greek alchemists for whom the devil is only "the aping shadow of God."[14]

The idea that one should imitate a "perfect" Christ who has chosen the good and the light and rejected evil and shadow has dominated our civilization. This type of relation to God, to the Self, is not necessarily useful at a psychological level. In his discussion of the concept of *privatio boni,* Jung criticizes the evolution of a doctrine according to which the sinister dimensions of the Self, of the *imago dei,* have been repressed:

> There can be no doubt that the original Christian conception of the *imago dei* embodied in Christ meant an all-embracing totality that even includes the animal side of man. Nevertheless the Christ-symbol lacks wholeness in the modern psychological sense, since it does not include the dark side of things but specifically excludes it in the form of a Luciferian opponent. Although the exclusion of the power of evil was something the Christian con-

---

13 "Christ, A Symbol of the Self," *Aion,* CW 9ii, par. 79.
14 "A Psychological Approach to the Trinity," *Psychology and Religion,* CW 11, par. 263.

sciousness was well aware of, all it lost in effect was an insubstantial shadow, for, through the doctrine of the *privatio boni* first propounded by Origen, evil was characterized as a mere diminution of good and thus deprived of substance. According to the teachings of the Church, evil is simply "the accidental lack of perfection."

Thanks to the doctrine of the *privatio boni*, wholeness seemed guaranteed in the figure of Christ. One must, however, take evil rather more substantially when one meets it on the plane of empirical psychology . . . .

If we see the traditional figure of Christ as a parallel to the psychic manifestation of the self, then the Antichrist would correspond to the shadow of the self, namely the dark half of the human totality, which ought not to be judged too optimistically. . . . The psychological concept of the self, in part derived from our knowledge of the whole man, but for the rest depicting itself spontaneously in the products of the unconscious as an archetypal quaternity bound together by inner antinomies, cannot omit the shadow that belongs to the light figure, for without it this figure lacks body and humanity. *In the empirical self, light and shadow form a paradoxical unity. In the Christian concept, on the other hand, the archetype is hopelessly split into two irreconcilable halves,* leading ultimately to a metaphysical dualism— the final separation of the kingdom of heaven from the fiery world of the damned.[15]

The notion of "paradoxical unity" is particularly important. The opposition between shadow and light within the Self should not be understood as resulting in a combat between the two poles. The *privatio boni* had been defined by Manicheism and Jung objected to being accused of having a "Manichean streak."[16] He takes sides neither with the Prince of Darkness nor with Light;[17] and, as opposed to the Manichean doctrine, he does not expect a redemption through which the individual would be delivered from darkness. On the contrary, he insists that the reality of evil should not imply a dichotomy and that shadow and light together characterize the unity of the Self. He observed that good and evil were begotten in the same way and remain brothers coexisting within the psyche;[18] they do not become

---

15 "Christ, A Symbol of the Self," *Aion,* CW 9ii, pars. 74-76 (emphasis added).

16 See ibid., par. 112n.

17 Jung did mention in his autobiography his "anxious hope" that meaning would "win the battle." *(Memories, Dreams, Reflections,* p. 359) We all tend instinctively to take sides with life and light. It would perhaps be absurd to renounce hope, even if it has to remain "anxious." Nevertheless, one may accept the contrasts good/evil, sense/nonsense, life/death and find peace; hope is the ego's own invention.

18 "God had two sons, an elder one, Satan, and a younger one, Christ. . . . if good and evil were begotten in the same way they must be brothers." ("Christ, A Symbol of the Self," *Aion,* CW 9ii, par. 103)

enemies and the Self accepts both. God had two sons, Lucifer and Christ, and, as a father, he could not have rejected one of them—at least psychologically speaking.

In these same pages, Jung remarks that the problem of the Antichrist is "a hard nut to crack" for anyone with a positive attitude toward Christianity. Elsewhere he stresses that it would not have occurred to him to advise the people who came to seek his help to leave the Church to which they belonged. However, it is a fact that for many people these Churches are no longer able to provide meaning. Their symbols and mythology have lost their numinosity, and the experience they offer does not correspond to the psychological needs of modern individuals. It is thus legitimate to wonder whether Christian doctrine in its present form corresponds in an adequate manner to the reality of the psyche and just where it conflicts with this reality. In other words, one may ask whether, in relation to the dark aspects of the Self, a "Christian attitude" is propitious psychologically.

If we find this attitude to be inadequate, then we must discover a way of confronting God's shadow without repeating the kind of dichotomy effected by the doctrine. How can we live in relation to the Self without breaking up its unity and turning its contents into two mutually exclusive principles? How is it possible to bridge the gap which, almost instinctively, we create between the two poles of the Self as we endow them with a value and attribute to them hierarchical priorities?[19]

I believe that, in confronting this gap, the analyst is faced with a temptation similar to that faced by the formulators of Christian doctrine, and may fall into the error of adopting a too one-sided perspective. The idea of a "positive healing" rests on a perception of the Self in which its total nature, including its irreducible duality, has been replaced by an attribution of the role of Savior to the positive pole. We may also say that the analyst risks introducing a dichotomy between the divine and the evil Self (between Christ and Antichrist), thereby forgetting a more basic perception (expressed by the duality inherent in the nature of the ancient Yahweh) which corresponds better to the true nature of the Self.

Obviously, a certain degree of optimism is useful in daily practice. The

---

[19] A historical distinction may be useful: the dichotomy and the repression of the negative pole do not stem from the original doctrine. In the Apocalypse, for example, the threatening side of God is still very much present; but, over the centuries, this perception has gradually moved into the background, at least as far as nonthe-ologians are concerned.

analytic profession does not choose explicitly to focus on the most sinister aspects of being. At a theoretical level, one should say that much of this is a question of definition and formulation. Logical thinking tends toward dichotomy and often defines through exclusion; it is not always easy to overcome this tendency. But the trap of too radical a dichotomy has a direct influence on the concrete work. Ideally, analyst and analysand need to find a propitious relation to both the dark and the light forces at work in the psyche. The attitude established by Christian tradition—that it is up to consciousness to triumph over evil and to control the dark shadows looming in the unconscious—does not correspond to psychic reality. It is far less adequate than the relation one may have to a divinity of the Yahweh type—a God acknowledged to be both loving *and* malevolent.

What is more, one should favor a form of thinking which accepts, both theoretically and in practice, that many phenomena connected to psychic reality inherently belong in the realm of twilight and shade rather than in bright daylight. In this sense, they are better characterized by formulations of paradox (Jung used the expression *and/or)* than by a polarization leading to a hierarchy of values. The idea of a *paradoxical unity* within the Self discussed above can only be grasped from this perspective.

Whichever terms one chooses, it is important to understand that, should "healing" take place, it will depend more on an attitude than on an answer. It will rest on experience, including mistakes and detours, rather than on the definition of a clear-cut path drawn by the positive pole of the Self. It is thus obvious that the relationship to Yahweh, or to the Christ-Antichrist totality, must be discovered individually, on a basis far more complex than it may at first seem. Here, again, absolute values do not exist. I am thinking, for example, of cases where what would be health for the majority is, for the individual concerned, a state of illness. Indeed, in some cases of "successfully treated" mental disease, patients have not only lost a large part of their individuality but also perceive life as less satisfactory and more painful than before.

Such examples show how nearly impossible it is to believe that light should win and that triumphing over the dark will bring about an ideal state. We have seen how problematic is the notion of "shadow integration." At the more global level of the Self and of the ego's relationship to a Godhead, another formulation may be more appropriate. There must be shadow so that there can be light—that is, to be divine, to be an adequate symbol of the Self, God must be endowed with a shadow.

But what about the notion of transformation and the aims often attributed to the analytic process? After all, very few people would be ready to work on something whose purpose has been negated in advance! Also, few would be ready to exchange well-established behavioral mechanisms, no matter how inadequate they have proven to be, for an approach in which no positive transformation in the collective sense can be guaranteed. The analysand must not, and cannot, resign; it is the hope of an existential change that prompted the decision to go into analysis.

Where, then, can this change take place? At the risk of being accused of playing with words, I would say that what needs to be transformed is not so much the contents of the psyche as the ego's relationship to them. The immutable, archetypal elements in the psyche cannot be transformed; but it is possible for the individual to relate to them differently.

My argument could also be put as follows. The true nature of God is irrelevant; it does not matter whether He is loving or not. What matters is to find a relationship to this God. The Self is given, manifesting in both the forces of life and death and, rather than trying to modify the balance of these forces, one should look for an attitude in which they can be both experienced and accepted. This obviously applies all the more to those cases where death and destruction dominate the psyche. At a practical psychological level, only this experience and the search for an adequate attitude matter; the rest is metaphysics.

In this context, we must come back briefly to a notion alluded to before, that of "value or nonvalue" as an integral part of the propitious attitude. (Jung knew very well how to apply it, beginning with his development of the association experiment.) An unpretentious attitude that attributes more value to experience than to objective results and renounces full control over what is right, what is wrong and what is valuable, may permit quite a bit of traveling, without the aim of the journey being known. It lets things happen organically, and it may allow a "nonvalue" to transform old elements and produce new ones more often than one may think. Sometimes, it is by looking for A that one finds a B that, at first, may seem to be a "nonvalue" but that will eventually turn out to be exactly what the psyche needed. This approach is closer to a certain form of animism (or at least to less rational perception) than to Logos-consciousness. It chooses to attribute primacy to the soul rather than to the progress implied by an Apollonian-type attitude.

With regard to analytic practice, this approach also implies a questioning and a partial rejection of the idea that our knowledge of the psyche is complete enough for us to decide what is absolutely right or wrong in a given situation. A pragmatic perspective is more appropriate; its apparent nonvalue acquires a value, not because it is intrinsic to a given action or idea, but because experience shows that it leads the individual further and allows for a renewed feeling of vitality. In that sense, the renunciation of the need to understand, evaluate and classify in advance may be the right approach.

Shifts

It may be useful to go back to what was said before about Christian doctrine, in order to elaborate on a number of ideas connected to the question of an adequate relationship to God and to the Self. The situation in which Westerners find themselves after centuries of Christianity must be better defined, and the place occupied by shadow aspects must be examined. In a society characterized by its associations with Christianity, the shadow of Christian doctrine—all the elements rejected, excluded or repressed by it—will run parallel to the shadow encounters forced upon the individuals who have been brought up in its context.

I would like to stress again that I am interested in the relationship to the (dark) Self rather than in a theological argument. The outline below follows Jung's reflections in *Aion,* with emphasis on those paragraphs concerned with the God-image in Christianity. I assume the reader is familiar with the chapters of *Aion* on the structure and modeling of the Self.

Jung emphasizes the discrepancy between the psychological experience one may have of the Self, in which the opposites including good and evil are reconciled, and traditional Christian doctrine where Christ stands for consciousness and good, while evil is attributed to Satan and the Antichrist. He also elaborates on his perception of Satan as the fourth aspect of the Trinity, whose inclusion would allow for a more complete image of God, corresponding better to the psychic reality of the Self.[20] In excluding a fourth element, or holding to a Trinity rather than developing a quaternity, doctrine represses the fourth to the level of the unconscious, and thereby fails to articulate a genuinely complete God-image.

Christ, on the other hand, is pictured by Jung as being at the center of

---

[20] See also, among others, "A Psychological Approach to the Dogma of the Trinity," *Psychology and Religion,* CW 11.

the only myth still alive in our civilization. In this myth, He plays the role of the hero, of original man, and even of eternal man. As this kind of divine totality, Christ images the archetype of the Self. The human soul is perceived as Christ's bride, in a perspective corresponding to that of the mystical wedding between Christ and the Church; this union has also been symbolized in the *coniunctio oppositorum* of the alchemists. The feminine—the anima—must have a place within a quaternity, whereas it had been excluded from the Trinity by Catholicism and limited to the one-sided figure of the Virgin Mary. It is characteristic of Christian doctrine that, in identifying the feminine with shadow aspects, it also fails to integrate it properly. But let us go back to the question of evil.

According to Jung, the refusal to accept the reality of evil in the shadow aspects of the Self leads directly to making human will responsible for it. Humanity is guilty whenever we fail to imitate Christ; we bring evil into existence since evil is nothing but a *privatio boni*, an inability to adhere to the good. But, in fact, we do not know what good and evil intrinsically are, nor can we define them in universally valid terms. They just are, in themselves and by themselves, and it is our consciousness that effects value judgments and enunciates moral principles.

When Christianity attributes the origin of evil to the human soul and makes the believer who does not succeed in imitating the perfection of Christ responsible for evil, it attributes a demonic power to the shadow. It banishes shadow and evil to the unconscious and connects them with the Antichrist. In so doing, it provokes a negative inflation and leaves the way open to *enantiodromia,* to an absolute swing in the other direction, since any unilateral attitude will tend to swing to its opposite. As a consequence of this pendular movement, Jung considers that our times (our aeon) may well see the end of the Christian era. But in many cases, for the individual in any epoch, the repression of the shadow in fact reinforces its power and always involves the risk that it will manifest in inadequate forms.

Over the centuries, the Christian message has stopped being fundamentally irrational and has been appropriated by reason. The intellect subjugated the psyche and the soul; technology subjugated nature. The "powers of the underworld" now hide under the mask of rationalistic ideologies.[21] According to Jung, Christian faith has, paradoxically, become the defender of the irrational. But its symbolism and in particular the image of Christ

---

[21] See "Transformation Symbolism in the Mass," ibid., pars. 444ff.

should be readapted to the reality of the psyche. In as far as it reunites conscious and unconscious, the Gnostic figure of Christ, corresponding to the original Christian tradition, may be included in a new image of the Godhead. However, psychologically speaking this approach may involve a risk of inflation because it presupposes an ego capable of resisting the temptation to identify with the Self or with its own image of "superior man." At this level, the importance of a propitious attitude becomes obvious: it should protect the ego from inflation, while avoiding both the repression of the dark and any dichotomy. As seen from the ego, this attitude should rest on an absolute respect for the forces involved, be they positive or negative, and thus on a reverence for the soul's awesome mystery.

The archetype of the Self is, indeed, far more complex and paradoxical than the image of the perfection of Christ would lead one to believe.[22] It is certainly not perfect and, if it is complete or symbolized by a totality, it is more in the sense that it comprehends a genuine humanness, with all the negative and maybe frightening aspects which are involved in this dimension. The development of consciousness has tended to replace an instinctive completeness (still sometimes to be found in children or in simple people) with a one-sided attitude in which certain aspects considered positive are privileged.

In this sense, completeness should be grounded in an ability genuinely to *be*, a capacity for being completely human rather than in a striving for perfection. It should thus rest on a perspective in which *every* aspect of the personality—and, further, of the Self—is given place. Here we come back to the importance of paradox, "I am this *and/or* that," without excluding or identifying with either extreme of a polarity.

We need to focus again on the nature of the Self, in order to stress that, beyond those aspects which have been split off in the image of Christ and attributed to the Antichrist, the Self also contains elements of the feminine, the chthonic and Eros. The alchemists understood this perfectly well, choosing to work on the transformation, through projection onto chemical substances, of the *prima materia* of the unconscious, including its chthonic aspects. They were in fact attempting to assimilate, directly and in a more complete manner than could the Christian doctrine of their time, an experience of the Self archetype in both its dark and light dimensions. This experience included the feminine, thereby compensating for an approach

---

[22] On the other hand, this image may be interpreted in a less one-sided manner than in the above sketch; we shall come back to this later.

dominated by the masculine and a male, heroic image of the Savior.

The tendency to repress the dark pole of the Self and to offer a positive vision of a rational, heroic man triumphing over evil in imitation of Christ runs parallel to the repression of the feminine in Western societies. But I believe that the inclination shown by Jung toward identifying sinister, shadow, unconscious qualities with the anima should be accepted only at a figurative level. It seems dangerous, and probably wrong, to equate "feminine" to "the female," or even to a concrete woman. However, it is first and foremost the so-called patriarchal religions that tend to eliminate the shadow aspects of the God-image. These aspects were much more present and accessible in those religions where goddesses, of the mother-daughter type in particular, played a central role. These religions also maintained a much closer contact with nature.

One may object that, in Jungian terms, the so-called primitive religions are essentially based on projection: psychic contents are projected onto nature and the social environment. They are then confronted externally, through ceremonies in which ritual and magic play an important role. But how much do we really know of how the individual experienced these ceremonies? Can we justify adopting an ethnocentric attitude and considering our religions to be of a higher order? And, even if we choose to attribute a great value to consciousness and thinking, does animism necessarily need to be relegated to the unconscious realm? I believe that it is possible to *consciously* adopt a religious perception closer to the matriarchal type.

Quite apart from this question and more to the point of our present discussion, the image of nature as being both nourishing and cruel constitutes a useful analogy for the Self. Nature is just what it is, and encompasses the two poles, positive and negative, life and death, transformation and destruction. In that sense, those religions which attribute a central importance to the relationship between man and nature may serve as a model for defining the propitious attitude toward the duality of the Self.

A discussion of the connections between the Self and the instincts would be helpful in this effort. Here, let us simply state that, by being better in touch with nature, matriarchal religions stand closer to the completeness of the Self. They include a chthonic element that, when incompletely projected onto a masculine image of God, risks remaining unconscious or regressing to an archaic level, with all the problems that then ensue.

Another essential aspect of the Self, again connected more to the irrational than to the rational, and to intuition more than to the spirit or Logos, is not properly symbolized by the image of Christ: the paradoxical dimension alluded to above in terms of *and/or*. Indeed, the Self is not only light and shadow, thesis and antithesis, or the force of opposition between irreducible elements. It is at the same time thesis, antithesis and synthesis, reconciling the opposites in a totality. We are dealing here with the transcendent function described by Jung. The polarizations good/evil, Christ/Antichrist are dangerous not only because they reinforce shadow aspects, but also because they hinder the discovery of a synthesis through the transcendent function, whose symbols express the true nature of the Self. In other words, the dichotomy good/evil and a one-sided identification with the positive pole exclude the possibility of the individual experiencing the transcendent function. Thus they exclude any access to the nourishing potential in the Self or to the discovery, on the part of the ego, of an adequate attitude toward its own crucifixion. This aspect has important consequences in practice since, according to the Jungian model, it is the transcendent function that carries the potential for healing

In brief, in order to discover the propitious attitude, we must allow chthonic goddesses to return, and we must also accept contradictions and paradoxes. The integration of these dimensions may well contradict a theological approach that looks for causes and furnishes absolute answers. But, psychologically speaking, this is the only possible attitude. Further, its completeness promotes a religious quest in the true sense. Jung draws out the basis for this in the following passage:

> Oddly enough the paradox is one of our most valuable spiritual possessions, while uniformity of meaning is a sign of weakness. Hence a religion becomes inwardly impoverished when it loses or waters down its paradoxes; but their multiplication enriches because only the paradox comes anywhere near to comprehending the fulness of life. Non-ambiguity and non-contradiction are one-sided and thus unsuited to express the incomprehensible.[23]

With regard to the present discussion, the acceptance of paradoxes may be expressed in an attitude that would include a rotation, a capacity to perceive both poles of the Self in turns, a circular movement choosing momentarily to focus on either the light or the dark, but never excluding one for the benefit of the other. We must find a way to accept "God's shadow" and live with it. We shall see later how this approach has been used by specific individuals and groups, as reflected in narratives, dreams or images that symbolize it.

---

[23] *Psychology and Alchemy,* CW 12, par. 18.

To anticipate later discussion I would stress that, beyond the problem of good and evil, this approach must also include the death archetype. Clearly, it is the Self and not the ego which decides on individual death, and it is the Self in both its dark and light aspects that eventually decides on the ego's death. This may explain why, as analysts, we find it so difficult to confront this dimension of the Self, why we would rather focus on its curative and integrative potential, and why we try to "integrate" the shadow, in the wrong sense. We are not only involved professionally, we are also concerned at a personal level. It may be easier for us to see our task as that of the "healer"—or at least of someone who can help to bring light and hope back into the analysand's life. This of course involves the risk of our identifying unilaterally with only one pole of the healer archetype.

More broadly speaking, it is easier for us to identify with life, or with what we mean by life, rather than to adopt an approach that embraces both death and life, in the paradoxical spirit appropriate to the archetype of healing.

3
The Life Ritual

Because the Self is endowed with a numinous nature, to relate to it one must enter into the religious dimensions of being. It is both within and outside the ego, constituting a field of psychic energy and transcending individual life. At a more psychological level, the Self *knows;* it is the archetype that may provide the individual with meaning and a place in the cosmos.[24] This being so, the quest involved in the analytic process naturally involves confronting questions that can only be termed religious, even when they are not concerned with theology as such.

For this to become clear, we need think only of the life/death duality as an integral part of the Self archetype. The confrontation with death always implies accepting a dimension that transcends consciousness and ego control and that raises the question of the meaning of life. The search for the propitious attitude must therefore take account of a religious axis. At this level, both analysand and analyst need to develop a relationship with the sacred, with the domain that relates to a transcendent power, including all the forms in which this power may manifest.

In order to define the means that can serve this confrontation, I shall reflect here on the way some social groups relate to the sacred. In particular, we shall see how they include both its light and dark sides in their perception of the cosmos, and how they develop ritual behavior designed to establish an adequate relationship with ambiguous deities. This type of behavior is most clearly expressed in rites of passage; these concern phases during which the sacred threatens to invade and destroy everyday life, since the passage involves a change in social order or a modification of personal status, depending on whether the rite is collective or individual.

There exist parallels between this type of ritual behavior and the manner in which individuals may effect psychic transitions. It thus seems useful to apply models developed by social anthropology to a psychological approach concerning modern individuals. But first we may view the prob-

---

[24] In what follows, I am using the contrast cosmos/chaos in the sense given to it by Mircea Eliade in *The Sacred and the Profane,* i.e., as equivalent to that between profane and sacred.

lem of the ego-Self relation from a more directly psychological perspective and ask what means are available to the ego for confronting the Self, both in its positive and in its negative dimensions. I could, of course, simply comment on Jung's ideas concerning the confrontation with the unconscious. This would include, among other things, a discussion of the transcendent function, and of the ways in which it manifests in symbols and in dreams. However, I am interested here in a much more specific problem, which may be formulated as follows.

Granted that in certain individuals the Self archetype has been unilaterally constellated, that is, that its dark pole overshadows the ego and that the ego-Self axis is inadequately developed, that it is unstable or even that it has been cut, where does the analytic process intervene to try to help the analysand manage the situation?

In my experience, work on dreams and personal symbolic material is often not possible at this stage or it does not help. In despair, the ego is either cut off from the unconscious or overflowed with negative material. It often cannot relate adequately to the symbols and may refuse to be touched emotionally. In this phase, it may thus be of help to use less personal material, encouraging the ego to step back and letting symbols emerge at a more transpersonal level. In the same sense, the whole analytic setting must encourage a passage through chaos (see below), into an imaginary world that is closer to deep layers of the collective unconscious. Through this passage a bridge will gradually be built, connecting the analysand with a more basically human level. The contact with archetypes may then give back to the individual psyche a sense of "being in the world," of being part of a larger cosmos.

Later in the process, this emotional experience can be brought closer to consciousness and to an ego that will have rediscovered its connectedness with the Self.

In other words, in cases where the ego-Self axis is lacking enough stability for a dialogue between personal conscious and unconscious, the analysis must first help the analysand regress (in the sessions) to the deeper levels of the collective unconscious where he or she may be nourished and strengthened by the Self. This will allow the axis to redevelop progressively and a dialogue between its two poles will become possible, allowing the analysand to confront more personal material.

Speaking more generally, individuation may be seen as a movement toward a greater awareness of the Self. Through the different stages of life, the ego constantly moves along what may be termed a Self-Self axis, that is, from the totally unconscious Self that preceded the stage in which the ego detached itself (ego-Self axis) to a more conscious Self, "conscious" being meant here as aware in an existential sense.

However, the movement toward greater Self-awareness is not a linear progression. The ego periodically regresses toward the original Self in order to bring back more elements from the (collective) unconscious. It is this movement that I believe analysis must accompany and guide—in every case, but when dark aspects of the psyche are constellated, this "return to chaos" becomes all the more essential. We shall see below how this return is effected by tribal man, for instance through ritual, and what the corresponding psychic mechanisms may be.

Imaginary Representations

The title of this chapter, "The Life Ritual," was chosen to express the central symbolic meaning in a short story whose motifs symbolize the way the ego may relate adequately to a transcendent dimension of life, to the Self. In the story a specific endeavor allows a moment of life to be created. Here is a summary:

> A teacher working for a short time in a countryside school notices that one of her students, a little boy of about ten, does not listen to the lessons. He daydreams and spends his free time writing in a copybook which he refuses to show her. He also won't let her talk to his parents. She is intrigued by the secret he seems to be hiding, but she does not insist on finding out what it is until the day when the boy breaks his leg by falling from a tree.
>
> The doctor wants the child to stay in hospital but he cries; he is in a state of absolute panic and insists he has to go back home, declaring that it is a matter of life or death. The boy eventually explains the reason for his upset: his parents are both dead and his only family is his grandfather, with whom he lives. Before dying, his father made him promise to take over his own daily task, that is to imagine and tell the grandfather every evening a new episode of a story. It is listening to this story that keeps the grandfather alive and, should the child fail only once in his task, the grandfather would die. Up until this day, the boy had conscientiously carried out his duty, despite the isolation involved by his not being able to tell anyone.
>
> The teacher promises to take the place of the child if he stays in hospital and invents a new episode for the grandfather, thus keeping him alive for another day.[25]

---

[25] From the British television series "Journey to the Unknown." The name of the author is not known, nor is the title it was given in the series.

Clearly, the story has a folktale-like character, and indeed one may find its pattern as a secondary motif in the index of *The Types of the Folktale* by A. Aarne and S. Thompson.[26] There, a person who is about to be taken away by the devil to whom he or she has sold his/her soul tries to gain time either by repeating a prayer or a story, or by baking bread. A similar motif is found in *1001 Nights:* having witnessed his beloved wife's adulterous behavior, the Sultan Shahriyar goes mad and kills one maiden after another after they have spent the night with him. Sheherazade, the Vizir's daughter, tells him (archetypal) tales—one every night. She is careful never to finish the story and thus, by sustaining his curiosity, keeps postponing his revenge until the next day. The parallel with our story is clear: death is being postponed by an act that feeds life, at a concrete or an imaginary level. In the Sultan's case, the tales even succeed in progressively healing his murderous impulses: after 1001 nights he finds that he has no longer any need to take revenge.

I see the story of the child with his grandfather as symbolizing a manner of approaching the dual nature of the Self, of relating to the archetype at all by granting it its proper place in everyday life. In fact, the relationship between child and grandfather, their mutual dependence and the solutions proposed by the narrative, leave many questions open. But, paradoxically, the use of an image to formulate a fundamental question already contains the germ of an answer. This approach is close to the transformation elaborated by the formulation of a rite: ritual work structures the chaos of being and thus modifies it, rendering it more accessible.[27]

As seen from a psychic viewpoint, the daily story imagined by the child and "fed" to the grandfather plays a specific role. It bridges elements belonging to both the conscious and the unconscious and, at a more general level, to the ego and the Self. Its function is akin to that of a ritual, whether we consider the time spent every day in storytelling as a rite or not. The child's imagination brings into the grandfather's life elements that can only be collective or suprapersonal; his stories have been told before, he cannot invent anything new. They allow the grandfather to remain connected to humanity in general, transcending his own individual fate. They

---

[26] See nos. 1199, "The Lord's Prayer," and 1199A, "Preparation of Bread."

[27] The expression "ritual work" was coined by ethnologist Victor Turner in *The Ritual Process: Structure and Antistructure*, referring to the term applied by the natives of Tikopia (see R. Firth, *We, the Tikopia*) to designate rituals: the "work of the gods."

keep him in touch with that part of the Self which is not only personal. I use the term "imaginary representation" to express the capacity of such a story to mirror a different reality and, thus, to serve as a bridge connecting ego and Self: the imaginary world is transpersonal, constituting a fluid, eternal source that transcends individual life; its images, on the other hand, find an echo in the individual's personal life experience and in the time-bound perception of reality.

Of course, the word "symbol" may also be used in this context. The tale told by the child will contain a succession of symbols; it will both express and impress, transforming energy and channeling it into a new form. But I use the other term in order to set it between the profane and the sacred, between linear and nonlinear time, as well as between directed and autistic thinking. What I mean by "imaginary representation" is the individual's active reception and physical or mental participation in images that are not a product of the ego only. No matter what means are used to do this, the images must be experienced emotionally rather than intellectually; their energy must touch the ego and provoke an affective reaction that will be a source of change. We shall see that, for instance, storytelling may work in a way similar to the way rituals work, by guiding the individual through a symbolic liminal period into a new state.

Henri Corbin wrote of the *mundus imaginalis:*

> There is a world that is both intermediary and immediate . . . the world of the image, the *mundus imaginalis:* a world that is ontologically as real as the word of the senses and that of the intellect. This world requires its own faculty of perception, namely imaginative power, a faculty with a cognitive function, a noetic value which is as real as that of sense perception or intellectual intention.[28]

James Hillman describes this imaginary world as a means of connecting with the archetypes, on the one hand, but also as a bridge toward a world in which the value of symbols results from their providing the individual with a "cosmic grounding."[29] In stressing the term "(imaginary) representations" and the importance of an active individual formulation of their contents, I am more interested in the pragmatic aspects of analytic work and less in the metaphysical—and up to a point socio-political—questions raised by Hillman.

---

[28] Quoted by Donald Sandner in his foreword to R. Ammann, *Healing and Transformation in Sandplay.*

[29] *Archetypal Psychology: A Brief Account,* pp. 2ff.

Let us go back to the child and his grandfather. The story contains two axes, time and imaginative power, and describes how the second works on the first, that is, how the ego may be able to apply the second in order to work on the first. To express this less abstractly, we can say that the child, by adding an episode to the narrative each evening, performs a ritual whose function it is to structure time and to create life. The ritual made into a tradition by his family allows a passage from profane, personal space to the sacred, transcendent space of images (the new episode) and this passage, by transforming time, creates a moment of life.[30]

On the other hand, the story does not mention the possibility of the grandfather living eternally; should this be the case, the new episode would have to be seen as functioning in a kind of automatic, mechanical manner: the old man would submit passively to his grandson's wish to keep him alive. As I understand it, the grandfather had to be curious enough to want to live until the next episode; he also had to be alive enough, or maybe "fed" enough by the last episode, to desire another day.

Rituals, in fact, act upon linear time, inescapable and quantified, which contains the life-death sequence, by feeding on time which is qualitative, by deriving nourishment from mythical time. After having examined how the duality sacred/profane manifests and is confronted in ritual, we shall focus on this dimension, since it constitutes the religious axis along which a genuinely healing analytic approach must orient itself.

Rites and Rituals

The expression *rites de passage* has been very much popularized, and sometimes applied in a loose manner. It may thus be useful to summarize briefly van Gennep's original description in *The Rites of Passage*.

At the core of such rites is a triphasic scheme: separation—liminal phase—reintegration. This simple notion reveals essential aspects and remains applicable in the case of any ritual ceremony, since van Gennep was explicitly more interested in describing forms rather than contents. Yet, almost every theory of ritual has been influenced by his description. Psychologically speaking, the triphasic scheme corresponds in fact to an archetypal sequence, that leading from death through transformation to a new life.

---

[30] The aspect "family tradition" may be interpreted as expressing the fact that meaning and values must find their roots "inside," in an inner world and within a continuity. (Thanks to Jean-François Vézina for this comment.)

However, the process of transformation may evolve not so much because a death automatically brings about a transformation and a resurrection, but because passages generally can be effected only if a period of marginality takes place. During the liminal phase, a reality that is outside society and culture—and outside ego life—is experienced. Deep values and emotions are brought into the open, put on a ceremonial stage and expressed in such a way that they may be accepted by the participants. Since this includes both mysterious and frightening elements, ritual work can be seen as allowing for a modification of negative polarities. During the ritual, the participants surrender their normal mode of perception and action. They scrutinize the values and axioms that have been chosen, among vast possibilities, to make up their culture and they thus come to a better acceptance of them. They also discover new dimensions. Ritual is a means of giving shape to something arbitrary (culture), but also of reinforcing it and of providing it with a dynamic aspect by periodically forcing the group to return to its roots.

In relation to the sacred—and thus to a religious axis—van Gennep defines rites of passage as "magico-religious practices" aimed at influencing natural events in such a manner that they cease to be dangerous.[31] They are always carried out when a passage between the profane and the sacred worlds must take place, that is, when a transcendent element influences everyday life. According to him, in tribal societies the sacred characteristically threatens to invade almost every domain of personal and social life. This would explain why these societies carry out so many rituals.

One may object to a perspective that implicitly sees tribal groups as less differentiated or less civilized than modern societies. I believe that, even in modern societies, the sacred manifests in every domain of life, except of course when we repress it because of a belief (!) in the absolute superiority of technology and science or because of a unilateral adherence to rational progress. Our lives are made up of a series of passages—life stages, passage of the days and of the seasons, but especially personal crisis and times of psychic anguish—and these passages always provoke an interaction between the sacred and the profane.

Most of what happens in ceremonies carried out by groups can be transferred to the individual level since the process in which a cosmos is being created out of chaos remains basically similar. However, one dis-

---

[31] *The Rites of Passage,* p. 13.

tinction may be useful: at the level of tribal groups, the term "ritual" is used to designate a clearly structured ceremony with a specific function; with regard to modern individuals, the movement profane-sacred-profane becomes part of a more personal quest and follows a rhythm that is not necessarily dictated by the group. And as far as analysis is concerned, it would be more correct to speak of a ritual-like behavior when referring to the regression to the Self that helps the analysand come to terms with its dark pole. Yet, both for the group and for the individual the passage through marginality involves contact with a religious dimension.

Myth and ritual are closely interrelated; that is, the myths that are particular to a certain tribe are enacted in the ritual. Thus, a given ritual is both a declaration about religion (this is what we believe) and a demonstration of its operation (this is how the gods work). In order to reach its aim, it proceeds in a very specific manner.

During the ceremony itself the "threshold people,"[32] that is, those going through the liminal phase, are moved outside the social and cultural network and therefore they escape classification. Their ambiguous and indeterminate position is expressed by a variety of symbols. A brief examination of some of these symbols, together with a description of actual contents found in the marginal phase, will provide a better understanding of the mechanisms involved at the group level. By analogy, it will also show what may happen during the phases of the analytic process in which the ego regresses toward the Self.

The novices are taken away from the village, speak in a secret language and must respect specific taboos. They may be classified with the spirits of their ancestors and painted black; they return to a cosmic state, letting their hair and nails grow and covering their body in mud or dust. The lose their identity, are robbed of their clothes and give up the name they had as children. Sometimes they are not allowed to speak, or only in a low voice. Other members of the tribe, quite often the women, are not allowed to see them. They are said to be embryos or babies, and must learn to walk, talk or eat again. The spirits must give birth to their new personality, and so they are given a new name. There is a constant coexistence of life and death symbols; the novices may be perceived as androgynous, or simultaneously human and animal. They are submitted to painful or frightening tests; this makes them malleable, ready for recreation. During the whole

---

[32] See Turner, *The Ritual Process,* p. 95.

marginal period they are taught practical skills and esoteric knowledge.

The ambiguity of the liminal period is underlined by the presentation of symbols that invert daily reality; the material world is turned upside down. This phase contains elements of playfulness and licence; everything becomes possible, the usual norms do not apply, and behaviors that potentially exist in everyday life may be experimented with. The novice must have confronted the chaos of the sacred to be able to accept the profane, and so the rituals are organized in such a way that, instead of eliminating the dangers inherent to a period of transition, they let these be shown and experienced very concretely.

For a brief period, the novice experiences the paradoxes of primeval being, like the Eskimo initiate "contemplating his skeleton," reduced to his own bones. The very foundations of life are systematically put in question; stimuli and symbols are fired at the individual in such a manner that he cannot defend himself. The novice must live simultaneously in opposite dimensions, experiencing extreme poles of being; he is being shown what is possible, while being taught what is approved. It is in this sense that the marginal period has a transformative potential: it contains all possibilities, contrasts them and opposes them to the negation of being that is potentially present in sacred chaos.

However, the sacred is not allowed to manifest in a totally arbitrary or uncontrolled manner. The ritual involves a conscious approach, having predefined its aims. The gods may be working through society as it performs its ritual duties, but the responsibility for the ceremonial acts rests in the hands of each group member. Because actions and consequences are made explicit, the message transmitted acquires validity. The ritual shows the invisible and interprets it through symbolization; it shows the unknown and refers it to what the novice knows. The ceremony does not end in the border state: the participants look the sacred in the face, but they immediately move back to the profane and integrate to it the elements discovered; there is a dialectical relationship between the two dimensions.

Ritual structures the cosmos and guides the individual from a state of passive submission to the group's tradition to a more cognitive acceptance of the sacred basis of culture. By analogy, the periods of psychic marginality, whether sought by the ego or imposed on it by the Self, may be seen as providing the individual with a better perception of place within the cosmos and a new interpretation of personal myth. This aspect is especially important to persons with a negative constellation of the Self archetype, for they may find meaning only if the dark elements are truly experienced and find a place within the ego's reality.

On the other hand, rituals help air and resolve ambiguities and conflicts. At the level of the group, by stating a given perception of the world, they integrate conflicting elements into a coherent world view and, by attributing a clearly defined position to each individual, they eliminate or channel the struggle for power. At the personal level, by helping one move to a less ego-centered perception, a passage through a similar process can help the ego endure tension and conflict and allow the transcendent function to be constellated. Existential questions are then no longer formulated in terms of either/or, and paradoxical solutions may be found by the psyche.

According to Rudolph Otto's essay on the divine,[33] man always has an ambivalent attitude toward transcendent aspects of life, since the powers involved are both benevolent and nefarious on the one hand, and not easily controlled on the other. The sacred is fundamentally given, both changing and immovable, and it remains unquestionable and unfathomable. It precedes humanity and contains us. It is only when societies elaborate a religious system and confront the transcendence of the sacred that it starts losing some of its ambivalent nature. Religions, by postulating an order, provide us with a basis from which to attempt to cope with the unfathomable. They establish causes and relationships, with respect to which prescribed gestures or practices are believed to provoke certain consequences.

The parallels with what happens at a psychic level in the relationship between the ego and the Self are obvious. The Self is given, is unquestionable and unfathomable, and it manifests an ambiguous nature, both benevolent and nefarious. Further, far from being only an ordering principle, the Self, like the sacred, is related to chaos; it pertains to nature and to the origins of humanity. It is a powerful entity which thinking and reason cannot simply structure and explain.

The contrast between profane and sacred may also be seen as a contrast between order and chaos. But this does not necessarily imply a separation of order from chaos: profane order remains part of a greater, sacred whole; it is a modified form of chaos, and the uncontrollable, unstructured sacred may at any time invade daily life and upset the control exerted by individuals. In a similar way, the ego is contained and related to the Self as a transcendent entity that may interfere with the control exerted by the ego.

---

[33] *The Idea of the Holy: An Inquiry into the Non-Rational Factor in the Idea of the Divine and Its Relation to the Rational.*

However, by discovering an adequate way of relating to the Self, the ego may find a way of coping and remaining in touch with a dimension that gives the psyche a place within the chaos.

Van Gennep writes that the sacred periodically "pivots on its own axis";[34] that is, whenever everyday structures are being changed, whenever a passage to another life stage needs to take place, one comes face-to-face with chaos. The sacred may invade the profane at any time. Any individual may be thrown back into a primeval, chaotic state which both contrasts with everyday life and transcends it, thus also broadening it. Psychologically speaking, this phase must be seen as an opportunity for the ego to find a better grounding and to relate differently to the dark aspects in the unconscious.

This ethnological digression may already have taken us too far from our topic. But there are striking parallels between the manner in which a tribal group finds the means to survive in a threatening cosmos and the way in which Jung sees the individual attempting to confront fate and move along the path of individuation.

With regard to the confrontation with dark aspects in the Self, the marginal period involves these aspects to a very great extent, and the novice must experience their power in an extreme form before being able to move on to a new stage. This dimension is particularly clear in shamanistic rituals: there, the novice must explicitly experience death, destruction and chaos. It is probably no coincidence that, over the past few years, so-called civilized people have rediscovered the form of initiation offered by such rituals. Indian medicine-men are brought to Europe, since Siberian shamans are not available.

Why this fascination? One possible answer may be found in the way our societies repress darkness; some individuals instinctively feel a need to compensate for this tendency and to experience the other pole in a dramatic manner, however questionable the organized mimicry of alien cultural forms.

The life ritual story recounted earlier in this chapter does not describe the manner in which the rite is carried out, except to say that the child has to narrate a new episode every day. On the other hand his stories are not specifically connected to the dark, but to the Self in all its aspects. Yet, he

---

[34] *The Rites of Passage,* p. 12.

does accomplish a ritual act, dictated by a family tradition, repetitive[35] and endowed with a specific function: in order to continue to live, the grandfather must be "fed" by his grandson's stories. If I imagine the scene taking place every night, I see it as surrounded by a serious, ceremonial atmosphere; it is not a sad event, but one in which both participants are aware of the importance of the moment.

Sacred Time and Psychic Reality

Eugen Bleuler defined a form of thinking that he termed "autistic-undisciplined" or "nonobjectivating" *(dereirend* in German) and of which he wrote that it tends not to adapt to reality and that it follows the "logic of feelings."[36] Later, he added:

> Among other things, it also serves to fill those gaps in our knowledge that we perceive as frightening. . . . It uses symbolism and drama in order to help us confront our inner conflicts and thus helps us toward a greater inner maturity and harmony.[37]

Bleuler's original distinction[38] was reformulated by Jung in his description of two kinds of thinking—"directed and adapted" or "subjective, actuated by inner motives."[39] In Jung's view, the latter is neither infantile nor pathological (as Bleuler suggested); its archaic nature is directly related to the "oldest layers of the human mind, long buried beneath the threshold of consciousness."[40] By analogy, this differentiation may serve to define more precisely the characteristics of profane and sacred time.

In more than one way, sacred time is situated within the realm of autism. It follows its own illogical and subjective paths and is related to the transcendent and the beyond, whereas profane time is linear, contain-

---

[35] It is one of the characteristics of rituals that they are repeated at regular intervals. For a broader theoretical discussion, see R. Rappaport, "Ritual Sanctity and Cybernetics"; Victor Turner, *The Ritual Process;* and the various articles in S.F. Moore and B. Myerhoff, eds., *Secular Rituals.*

[36] "Das autistiche Denken" [Autistic Thinking].

[37] *Lehrbuch der Psychiatrie* [Textbook of Psychiatry], pp. 41-42 (my translation).

[38] This distinction also involves a contrast in the way each of the brain's hemispheres function, or at least was seen to until recently. See K.W. Bash, "Hemisphärenharmonie" [Hemispheric Harmony]; it seems that neurologists have now modified their theory concerning a clear segregation of tasks between the hemispheres.

[39] *Symbols of Transformation,* CW 5, pars. 37ff.

[40] Ibid., par. 39.

ing its own beginning and end. The god Cronos clearly symbolizes the duality of time—directed/autistic, linear/random, profane/sacred—when he is represented with four wings, two of which are outspread as if he were about to take flight, while two are lowered as if he were resting. The two pairs of wings symbolize the passage of time on the one hand, and the ecstasy of transport beyond time on the other. They symbolize the contrast between the continuity of past-present-future and the simultaneity of the eternal.[41] The "second face of Cronos" (he is sometimes depicted with four eyes, two in front and two behind) thus personifies an autistic time that is infinite, with no beginning, end or direction. It symbolizes a dimension of sacred time that can be grasped only in an approximate manner.

The kinship between the Self and sacred time is fairly obvious. Both have a subjective, unfathomable dimension, and both are subjectively motivated, that is, they follow their own internal logic. Both *just are,* without any reference to norms or value systems situated outside their field. In the Self, as we have seen, each component has a value only as it is assigned by the ego, and not intrinsically. As for sacred time, it precedes and stands beyond any linearity and, thus, any kind of hierarchy.

Mircea Eliade, in *The Myth of the Eternal Return,* writes of the *illud tempus,* of "that time" at the beginnings of the cosmos when everything was being created and through which everything will be recreated. He adds that, as societies move toward more consciousness, they tend to attribute a more historical, more linear dimension to time and to move away from the "initial time," from the mythical beginnings of the creation. Profane time would thus be historical, while sacred time is a-historical. For Eliade, rituals help the group reconnect with the totality, with the wholeness of the *illud tempus.* They could thus be seen as an attempt at participating, be it only for a limited time, in the original unconscious within which thinking and experience surrender directedness in order to be nourished by images and autistic motifs.

Put otherwise: rituals are a means of contacting the divine child, Jung's "initial and terminal creature."[42] The contact with sacred time and its images also provides the individual with the means to participate in a suprapersonal, eternal psyche. This participation, this "eternal return" through ritual to mythical origins, provides us with the knowledge that we are not

---

[41] See J.E. Cirlot, *A Dictionary of Symbols,* p. 65.
[42] See "The Psychology of the Child Archetype," *The Archetypes and the Collective Unconscious,* CW 9i, pars. 259ff.

alone. It thus allows us to face the dark aspects of the sacred—and of the Self—without suffering more than necessary and without the pain provoked by isolation: we are supported by the awareness that many others have had this experience.

Let us go back to our fantastic story, as an image of the way in which a return to the *illud tempus* may be effected and may bring about a renewal of life. Because the child "imagines," in the strongest sense of the word, the grandfather is able to reach past linear, biological time and to connect with the "whole man," feeding on a transcendent dimension. Intrapsychologically, since the two figures must be seen as two aspects of the same psyche, a vital element (the child) and an active commitment (in which the daily episode, as an imaginary representation, allows for a connection with the sacred) make it possible for the whole psyche to live along a religious axis that transcends the individual level and the linearity of time.

Cronos simultaneously shows his two faces. The child and the grandfather spend most days in a linear reality, but each also works at maintaining a contact with the sacred dimension of time. They are thus both able to feed from the original wholeness and to find a place in the cosmos.

Of course, the contrast between profane and sacred times may also be seen as a contrast between the conscious and the unconscious. We would then have three (not equivalent) pairs: directed/autistic thinking, conscious/unconscious and profane/sacred.

My basic hypothesis is as follows: by resting at the junction of each of these pairs, "ritual work"—this term being applied here both to traditional ceremonies and to a regression along the ego-Self axis—makes it possible to overcome their dualities or, rather, to situate them within an equilibrium that is otherwise threatened by the tendency to dichotomize and to attribute primacy to logical thinking, to technology and to the Logos version of progress.

I have used the expression "imaginary representations" to designate those aspects of the ritual work that may support a healing. In terms of Jungian psychology, they include the contents of the personal and collective unconscious, dreams and their symbols, folktales and myths, etc. Technically speaking, they may be accessed by a form of active imagination (representation). At a more basic level, they can be understood as a function of feeling and of affective needs, as in Bleuler's autistic thinking. It may be that we are no longer fluent enough in speaking the corresponding language. We have lost contact with that form of thinking and with the symbolic aspect of daily events. Instead, we tend to use clever, clear formulations to describe and rationalize our cosmos.

Yet, in order to remain connected with the religious axis discussed above we must be able to relate to the half-light of images that express more than they say. I sometimes feel that too much value is being attributed to the light of "consciousness," at least as far as the analytic process and its existential dimension goes. Theorizing is one thing, relating to the unconscious and understanding the language of the psyche is quite another.

Jung was searching for an equilibrium between conscious and unconscious or, even, was pleading for a reevaluation of the unconscious. It seems to me that it is dangerous to put too much stress on aims such as "broadening consciousness," for this risks telling dreams what they mean rather than listening to their message and watching the ego's emotional reaction. What is more, we analysts sometimes create an artificial border between conscious and unconscious by isolating the symbolic material that crosses our path, by treating it within a closed system of interpretation. In other words, we may, paradoxically, dichotomize too much the pair conscious/unconscious.

Further, I believe that we tend to concentrate too much on explaining and interpreting, as if this were the ultimate aim of analysis, while the need of an analysand may be just as much to reconnect with the marginal characteristics of the sacred and the unconscious.

We do need models for thinking about the analytic process and structuring it. However, what happens *within* the process must be of an emotional, existential nature and, at this level, explanations and models are useless. What is more likely to bring healing is a transference-countertransference relationship allowing the analysand's ego to connect with psychic reality, and in particular with the original chaos in which one's individual cosmos may be (re)anchored. This vital process cannot be contained within a rational vocabulary. Its verbalization may even inhibit the emotional reactions that are essential both to the transference-countertransference and to the passage through a marginal phase, outside the ego world.

Michael Fordham writes that "archetypal reactions" form the basis of the analytic technique.[43] Archetypes, in a Jungian sense,[44] are, obviously,

---

[43] "Notes on the Transference."

[44] In *The Myth of the Eternal Return,* Eliade uses the term with a different meaning: to designate the model used by the gods at the time of creation.

an integral component of the sacred time that renews the profane—and of Hillman's *mundus imaginalis*. Fordham's archetypal reactions are thus a means of contacting and relating to this time, in both its friendly and its nefarious dimensions. The sharing of the transference-countertransference relationship provides the analytic process with a liminal dimension and this is particularly important with regard to the confrontation with the dark Self. Under the analyst's guidance, the analysand can pass from a personal to a transpersonal level, away from a feeling of being isolated and into a more generally human experience. Instead of being a prisoner of the contrast between his or her own suffering and the norms of happiness defined by society, the analysand is able to return safely to the very source of human sorrow, to the dark and threatening dimensions of being.

If we accept that marginality allows the rites of passage to achieve their aim, then we should be prepared to accept that healing will, of necessity, involve marginality. Healing thus also involves the reversal of profane reality and the return to *another* time characteristic of that phase. Moving away from the profane implies moving away from its norms and from a collective, ego perception of reality. Is it so wrong, then, to postulate that it is by deliberately swimming against the current, by refusing to be influenced by collective norms of progress and transformation, that the individual may be healed? It is by accepting the dark, the ugly, the sick that we may succeed in being faithful to the true nature of the soul. And we need to accept chaos so as to maintain a contact with the sacred and thus with the religious axis indispensable to a healthy psychic vitality.

More generally speaking, a passage through the liminal aspects of the unconscious provides an experience that is essential to individuation. According to Jung, the individual stands between the conscious and the unconscious part of the collective psyche. Individuation should not be taken to mean only "becoming more oneself" and going, so to speak, against the collective. It also involves fulfilling a function within that collective, finding a place there:

> Every mental or moral individuality differs from all the others, and yet is so constituted as to render every man equal to all other men. Every living being that is able to develop itself individually, without constraint, will best realize, by the very perfection of its individuality, the ideal type of its species, and by the same token will achieve a collective value.[45]

---

[45] *Two Essays on Analytical Psychology,* CW 7, par. 504.

As we have seen, the function of rites is not only to make the sacred chaos less dangerous or less painful. Ritual action is also a search for the nourishment and renewal provided by the suprapersonal wisdom of the sacred world. This element is clearly shown, for instance, in the Biblical story of Jonah's journey in the whale: he cuts the whale's heart and eats it. At this level, marginality may be closely related to the manifestation of the transcendent function. A contact with collective experience and with the objective psyche allows elements to be discovered that the profane ego is unable to see. During the marginal phases, by moving away from the tensions resulting from the various norms and alternatives faced by the ego, and by surrendering ego control, the individual allows the psyche to take the lead. In so doing, one may discover ways of "best realizing the ideal type of its species," that is, of becoming more human.

It is always very difficult to escape the value judgments dictated by cultural norms, since culture is mainly unconscious. By referring to ethnological theories, I have tried to escape some of the determinism of my own Western thinking and to situate the problem outside of the dichotomies enforced by Christianity. The elements that have been discussed here as characteristic of the confrontation with sacred time through rituals can be seen as components of a specific attitude toward that dimension of being. In a later chapter, they will be expressed in terms of components in the propitious attitude toward the Self and its darkest energies. This attitude, by bridging the gap between sacred chaos and profane order, may serve to give each individual a *place* within a cosmos that includes them both, rather than providing one with a certainty about the *meaning* of life, a certainty that would, after all, be rather fortuitous.

Before closing this first, theoretical part and moving to a discussion of more pragmatic and symbolic aspects, I cannot resist quoting a beautiful passage from a text by Sheila Moon. Its images very adequately show what is involved in individuating:

> The Ashanti of Africa . . . believed that the Creator gave a bit of his spirit to everyone whom he sent to earth, and that with the gift of that bit of spirit— the man's soul—was bound up that man's destiny, what he was to become and to do in the world. . . .
>
> [What we need to do] to fulfill our own destiny as creatures, is to be as rich, as total in our unique humanness as a tree in its treeness. Yet one further step is needed from us which the tree does not have to take. For the tree has not lost itself, since from the beginning it has been humbly obedient to its particularity. Not so with us. We have become confused in the cerebral labyrinth of whence and whither. We have sought to be more than human—

that is our greatness—but have insisted on our own definitions of how—and this is our littleness.

If we can but learn, as this myth shows, the simple and hard lesson of emergence, of going into the darker places to follow the restless longing upward, of letting no small thing stay forgotten and unhonored, then we shall be whole. Then we shall be related to the unconscious powers within us of life and God. This is redemption.[46]

---

[46] *A Magic Dwells: A Poetic and Psychological Study of the Navaho Emergence Myth,* pp. 181-183.

Part Two

A person with the Beginning Gift of the Mind must always try to
include his Heart in his decisions. . . . A man can live out
his entire life without ever finding more than what was already
within him as his Beginning Gift, but if he wishes to Grow
he must become a Seeker and Seek for himself the other Ways.

—Hyemeyohsts Storm, *Song of Heyoehkah.*

4

Practice

Although I am mainly interested in the practical aspects of analytic work, it was my concrete experience with analysands that inspired the foregoing theoretical reflections. They have nourished my daily work with clients and been fed in turn by new experiences. It thus seems appropriate to present a few examples drawn from practice.

This presentation is not unproblematic. The work involves intimate aspects—for the analysand, but also for the analyst—which should be respected. It is not sufficient to disguise the identity of the people concerned. Indeed, the discussion of a case always brings a disturbance in the process, in that it modifies the vectors of tension within the transference-countertransference. A movement of libido takes place, greater in the unconscious than at the conscious level, and has a rebound effect on the analytic process. We may say that, in the analytic relationship, the whole that is made up of conscious and unconscious—both personal and collective—is like a complex mobile, resting in a state of delicate balance.[47] Whenever one point of this mobile is displaced, or simply touched, the whole structure vibrates and a movement may occur at a very different point or rebound to where the mobile was first touched. I do not believe that this influence is always positive, even when the analytic work as such is finished.

In addition, a large part of what happens in the analytic vessel is of a purely nonverbal nature; it is fluid and not easily translated into words. A case discussion may provide objective data on the client, it may try to describe the atmosphere in which the exchange took place; but it will never give an adequate description of the (al)chemical reactions that have typically influenced the analytic process. These belong as much to the affective realm as to the world of symbols or archetypes, and affect is always subjective.

Because of these problems, I have had to find equivalents for biographical data as well as for some dreams. I have also synthesized two cases into one. In other words, the actors or the events of my analytic practice have served only as models for the following sketches.

---

[47] This image was suggested by Sonja Marjasch, Jungian analyst in Zürich.

In discussing cases here, I would also like to show certain defense mechanisms available to the psyche when it needs to protect against the constellation of the negative pole of the Self. We shall see in chapter five which archetypal schemas may serve to compensate for these various ego attitudes. However, where the soul is concerned nothing is simple. One specific defense mechanism or its compensation in the unconscious may become more apparent, but each of the processes discussed is made of a complex network of conscious and unconscious reactions. What is more, an ego that feels cornered may do all that is in its power not to have to face the dark, and thus will move to another stratagem as soon as it is no longer able to defend in the old way.

I am not trying to play down the difficulties met by these analysands. It is never easy to face the shadow and, in their case, the confrontation is made harder by the fact that at an archetypal level the shadow of the Self is also constellated. Meeting the dark Self is generally an extremely frightening, numinous experience; it may lead the ego to believe that it is going to be destroyed and it is only natural that it will try to defend. Often, the analysands experience it as the act of a malevolent God and feel absolutely helpless. They may also believe unconsciously that they are not "normal," that is, that they are unable to meet the norms of a society that, indirectly, is telling them: "If you are not able to triumph over the negative and to eliminate your despair, you are not one of us." It is thus no wonder that they resort to all sorts of defense mechanisms.

Broadly speaking, mechanisms that allow the ego to avoid facing the negative pole of the Self can take one of three forms, corresponding to three different attitudes: denial of the negative, passive resistance and identification. More specifically the ego's reaction may be withdrawal, indifference, inflation (positive or negative), rebellion or regression (or even psychosis, as an attempt to return to the original Self).

Here is a brief summary of the consequences of each attitude for the individual psyche and its mode of adaptation in everyday life.

Denial of the negative. The ego may withdraw and become indifferent to the Self, repressing it into the background. The analysand may then have a feeling of inner emptiness, caused by being cut off from the unconscious. Or the ego may deny the negative in a paradoxical manner, that is, look systematically for the positive which—it hopes—will provide a stronger grounding. In both cases (withdrawal or paradoxical avoidance) the negative may emerge in the form of psychosomatic symptoms. In the second case, the analysand will have the tendency to idealize positive values in a rather inflexible manner, quite often adhering to an ideology justifying this tendency, be it a religion or some other belief system.

Passive resistance. Here the ego protects itself by projecting or delegating the negative. I am using the term "passive resistance" because the psyche trapped in this mechanism does acknowledge the existence of the negative, but keeps a distance from it by attributing it to someone else. The partners of alcoholics or drug addicts come to mind, since in quite a number of cases it is the need for projection or delegation that keeps them in a relationship which appears to cause suffering. Certain forms of life refusal also belong in this category: in order to prevent the negative from influencing everyday life, the individual lives below his or her level. Apart from the fact that this attitude also prevents the positive from manifesting, it corresponds to a partial suicide, since part of the personality is cut off.

Identification with the negative. This may bring strong aggression, both self-directed and toward others. In individuals where the ego boundaries are not very strong, this may lead to obsessional states: the world is perceived exclusively in its darkest aspects. In other cases, the ego may undertake a compulsory—often sublimated or intellectualized—quest for the negative Self. This may include a kind of flight forward, in which the ego longs for disintegration in death. Accordingly, suicidal tendencies are quite frequent.

All these defense mechanisms make it impossible for the ego to dialogue with the Self or to experience clearly its negative pole. Inflation distorts everything. And the negative occupies more space and uses more energy than would be required were the ego to accept its presence.

Heart with No Companion

During our first session, Miguel tells me that he wants to do analysis because he must "find the road away from" his family. He had tried, but each time found himself blocked and returned to his parents. More recently, a number of traumatic events—the accidental death of a close relative, the break-up of a relationship with a woman—have confused him tremendously. He feels "totally lost, like an adolescent who is afraid of everything," despite his twenty-five years. He appears to suffer from melancholy rather than from a genuine depression; but he has trouble concentrating and he presents a number of psychosomatic symptoms.

Miguel is the youngest of twelve children. His parents are foreign workers who find hope in the hard work that will allow them to go back to their country and build a house there. The couple seems harmonious, but there is a lack of communication between them: both work too hard and, besides, they have never learned to express their feelings. The mother is very religious; she has attempted to inculcate extremely strict moral and Christian principles in her children. The father has had to give up his professional ambition and—as is often the case in immigrant families—has transferred it to his children. Miguel describes his childhood as happy: he was a contented child who always smiled and was spoiled by his older brothers and sisters. Together, they make up a real tribe, for whom solidarity is very important. Even with the older siblings out of the home and married, they all meet every Sunday to share a traditional meal.

Under this apparently harmonious surface, Miguel's parents have, literally, not had enough to feed their children, at least the youngest ones: three of them have psychic problems. The very traditional values they have been taught do not leave much space for their individual personality; they are also poorly adapted to their cultural environment. For a long time, Miguel managed to make his way, supported by the model chosen by his parents. He received good technical training and found work he likes, although this has meant surrendering the more artistic side of his personality. But he feels a stranger outside his family; he is isolated between two cultures and does not feel he really belongs to either. He is also a perfectionist, both with himself and with others. Now that he is grown-up, he says he is unable to feel pleasure or to have satisfying relationships. He has started criticizing his mother's strict ideas and as a result is both fascinated and terrified by the new world that opens itself to him. A short relationship with an older woman, especially, has helped him discover a whole new realm of imagination and (dark) sensuality. After their relationship ended, he did not know how to cope with those aspects of himself she had helped him discover.

Miguel first applied the patterns he was familiar with to the analysis: he invested great amounts of energy and expected results in return, "progress" in the collective sense. He was very motivated and thought constantly about his problems. His unconscious, however, was more reticent and only started expressing itself after a number of months. But his first series of dreams were quite forceful. Here is one:

> I am in my parents' house, in the kitchen, together with my father and a few of my brothers and sisters. Our cat, a young, playful animal, has been locked

into a box. An old woman whom I don't know takes the box and wants to kill the cat. I try to defend the kitten and start a physical fight with her. She is awful-looking, with twisted limbs, but she is also terribly fast. I am scared. There is blood everywhere.[48]

Life, the new life Miguel had discovered with his girlfriend, is threatened by a witch; he actively tries to fight her, but he is not sure he will win. What is more, the kitten is trapped (his association was: "It is something my family would do") and this makes it easier prey for the witch. Around the same time, Miguel spontaneously painted a picture in which the witch is depicted as a panther, "terribly wild and cruel, but also extremely beautiful." Both the witch and the panther he associated with his former girlfriend. His unconscious insisted on another aspect of the motif:

My brother is very sick. He is crying and he refuses to leave the house; he has closed all the shutters. He is convinced that he has murdered a little girl. I go back home to talk with him. Someone says that the body has been buried in the garden. I start digging in the ground.

The brother, the shadow of the ego, is the one who, during these weeks, genuinely suffered. In his everyday life and in our work, Miguel continued to be quite active; but in some sessions he also looked almost indifferent and started withdrawing. He relentlessly sought rational solutions to his problems. When talking about the dream, he said he felt responsible for his brother, but did not know how to comfort him. Anyway, he said, his brother should start thinking and realize that all of this was pure nonsense. He assured me that his own problems were far less serious and began describing his ideals and his projects for the future in a tone (that of his mother's animus, I suspected) that did not tolerate any contradiction. Still, he was on his way and slowly opening to the dark elements that had been repressed. In one of his dreams, he was fighting alongside an Australian aborigine whom he associated with "nature and the instincts"; he was actually pleased that he had taken the aborigine's side. Soon after, he met a girl he had known when he was an adolescent and this meeting reactivated his latent depression.

During the following months, Miguel gradually slid into what he described as "an abyss." He was able to keep his job, but he spent all his spare time alone at home. He painted and kept a diary; most of the time he

---

[48] This dream, like all the others below, has been simplified, so that no acquaintance with the dreamer's biography is needed for understanding; this explains its somewhat schematic quality.

was unable to do anything and sometimes, he reported, even unable to move. At times he actually lost contact with reality; he had hallucinations and heard voices. He was still coming regularly to the sessions but complained that "this will lead nowhere."

Later during these months, Miguel became obsessed by a woman (Ruth) he had met recently and with whom he wanted to have a relationship. She was not interested in him and he oscillated between anger and despair; he wanted to force her to love him. Ruth came from a social milieu that was very different from his own and she personified all the elements that had been repressed by the strict principles adhered to by his parents. During these critical months, she was constantly "with" him: he talked to her in his head, wrote her letters which he did not send, hid near the school where she worked in the hope of seeing her, if only for a second. At other times, Miguel felt persecuted by her invisible presence. She was the anima that may guide him, but during this period he often saw her as a cruel witch. Eventually, a dream made a big impression on him:

> Ruth has had a child, a little boy. I know that he is my son.

For the first time, Miguel did not attempt to rationalize. He was deeply moved and, after first wanting to write Ruth a letter to beg her to accept him, he understood the message from the unconscious: Ruth, the "witch" who lives in a world so different from that of his parents, now shows him the way to a new life, giving him a child he will have to bring up.

From this time on, the whole atmosphere of the analysis changed. Miguel gave up his rational argumentation and progressively came out of his depression. Outside of the analysis he became less isolated; he began to take risks and to accept making mistakes. He used to keep trying to find his way by using sheer will power, striving for his ideals by investing huge amounts of energy he did not really have. Now he allowed himself periods of rest, of waiting.

He demanded less of himself but, paradoxically, he was more successful and a number of positive events reflected a renewal of vitality. A dream depicted his new existential situation quite appropriately :

> I am on a ship, a sailing boat floating on a very blue sea. We are getting closer to an island and I see on the beach a house that is exactly my dream house. But there are guns on the beach and someone shoots at the boat, missing it. I am afraid. I have weapons, many weapons, and I consider landing and conquering the island. But instead I sail the boat around the island, beyond the reach of the guns. We are sailing in concentric circles, waiting.

I have no doubt that Miguel shall, one day, find a place where he will feel at home. In a more recent dream, he was sharing his flat with Ruth and this seemed perfectly natural to him.

Setting aside an interpretation in terms of integrating the anima, the aspect in Miguel's case that seems important to our reflections is that of the evolution of his relationship to the elements that had been dichotomized during his childhood. This evolution took place under circumstances that were relatively dangerous for the ego, since more than once he came very close to psychosis. Other details of his biography might support the hypothesis that he had to carry a heavy psychic inheritance, which his parents managed to pass on without being affected themselves simply because they had stuck with collective values. The shadow and destructive aspects had accumulated all the more energy and flooded Miguel with great violence. But, in his case, it was this frightening regression, this true "descent to hell," that allowed a healing to take place.

On the other hand, when Miguel's strict values (that had prompted him to identify with ideals such as goodness, success, work and reason) were shaken—by external events on the one hand, and by the obscure intuition that moved him to look for life outside his family on the other—the repressed energies erupted with frightening force. He was then compelled to surrender the attitude which, until then, had allowed him to succeed—at least on the surface—and to discover that he might also be able to reach his aims by letting life carry him rather than by fighting—by sailing in circles rather than by conquering, in the image of the above dream. He learned to move without damage within the realm of his fantasy; he also discovered that he has a genuine sense of humor. He once described the analytic process like this: "I used to want a super-jet that would take me to a wonderful country. Now I am slowly driving my little jeep on a country road."

Miguel has stopped being afraid when he cannot find the way back to his parents' house. He actually has fewer contacts with the "tribe" and no longer feels guilty about it. He is able to live his own life and he is better armed to fight against the giants and the witches he still meets. But, more important, he is on the move and, insofar as the work with the unconscious allowed him to discover Eros, he has found the vitality whose lack caused him so much pain.

Far into adulthood Miguel had been an adolescent lost in a kind of schizoid isolation: he could not find a direction, had great trouble remaining in contact with his feelings and could not use his potential to the full. Mainly, he felt very much alone and lacked vitality. For various reasons, he had not made contact with that transcendent entity that could contain and guide him. Despite the warm atmosphere of his family, he did not feel supported by life; he was scared of the dark aspects he intuitively perceived under the harmonious surface; he was blocked and later, during the analytic work, he came dangerously close to psychosis.

Yet, the passage through this very difficult phase freed Miguel and he found a new orientation. He very concretely experienced despair and was able to avoid a tremendous regression only because his ego was, in spite of everything, stable enough and constantly prompted him to keep looking. Nevertheless, in a case like this the analyst's function is indeed to accompany the psyche through a number of negative, shameful and confusing steps, so that it can rediscover its roots and reactivate its creative potential.

The Witch's Brew

The psychic problems that in Miguel's family had been repressed into the unconscious were only too manifest in Vivian's. Her father is an alcoholic who, when she was a child, only came home to quarrel violently with his wife. Her mother suffers from serious depressions and has tried more than once to kill herself. A terrible childhood, then, during which Vivian had to grow up very fast: she was the one who took care of the housework and looked after her two younger sisters. And yet, on the surface, these difficult times do not seem to have left any scars.

Vivian left home relatively early; she did an apprenticeship, then went to night school and finally to university. She is successful in her profession and has been living for a number of years with a man she loves very much. She is now over thirty, but still has the face of a young girl, smooth and innocent-looking: a *puella* who has not become a woman. She tells me she wants to do analysis because she is "absolutely exhausted." Acute problems have interfered with the relationship to her male friend; she suffers from chronic stomach pains, as well as from amenorrhoea. She feels generally depressed and scared.

One of her first dreams describes the tension tearing at her under her apparent balance:

> During a holiday spent in Spain with my boyfriend, we go to a restaurant. I am looking for the toilet and go down to the cellar. The stairs are shaky and dirty, but I am desperate to go to the toilet. The more I descend, the more I

find myself deep in mud and excrement; the bodies of dead animals are floating on top of this and the level is rising. I have more and more trouble moving and I can hardly breathe.

On the outside, all is fine: Vivian associates Spain and the restaurant with happy times in the relationship. But in the unconscious, things are very different. Although consciously she considers hygiene to be very important, filth, dirt and corpses threaten to choke her. Taking into account her past, the problem may be formulated as follows: as a child, Vivian had reacted to her difficult situation on the one hand by escaping into a world of fantasy (the *puella),* and on the other by actively playing the mother role. Protected by the cocoon it had woven in response to external events, her ego had gained considerable strength; this stability had allowed her to survive and even to achieve a lot. But she had become like a soldier who keeps going to battle; she had worked, studied and cared for others, determined not to be beaten by circumstances.

This defense mechanism had served her well for quite a long time; but it had cut her off from her own chthonic, instinctive nature (in the dream, the excrement and the corpses underground) and, to some extent, from her femininity. What is more, through being repressed for so long, these elements had gained in power and were threatening to stifle her.

The motif of repressed shadow due to a one-sided identification with positive values is clearly expressed in the following dream:

> I am in the house where I lived as a child; the walls have partly caved in, rain is coming in. Mrs. X is sitting on a chair. I try to talk to her but she does not react at all. She is looking very scared, as if paralyzed. Suddenly I find myself in Mrs. Y's house. I have the feeling that I am doing something that is forbidden, and dangerous. I am afraid and do not know any longer where to go.

Mrs. X is a distant relative greatly admired by Vivian. She manages her own business; she is always dressed very elegantly and "does and says what she wants." Mrs. Y is a very old woman who lived in the village where as a child Vivian spent her holidays. Rumor had it that Mrs. Y was a witch who was able to do black magic; she had little contact with the rest of the villagers but Vivian got on very well with her and Mrs. Y even became a kind of surrogate mother for her. The two women symbolize the two poles that in Vivian have been in conflict. Up until now, she has chosen Mrs. X as her ideal: she works hard and shows herself in her best behavior, although, unlike Mrs. X, she often does what is approved by others rather than what she really wants. Mrs. Y, to whom Vivian feels closer emotionally, has been repressed and disapproves of her.

In the following months, a series of dreams depicted her dark side more clearly: Mrs. Y is a wild woman, close to nature; she may get into fits of terrifying rage and sometimes she will break up everything around her. But she is also the one who knows the secrets of plants and how to concoct healing brews. Vivian feels these forces in herself, the rage, the unrestrained feelings, the natural wisdom, but she has never allowed herself actually to use or express them. She sees them as irrational and, in a way, immoral: they remind her too much of her parents' chaotic world. The energy symbolized by Mrs. Y may "knock mountains over"—in a negative as well as in a positive sense—and she is afraid of it. She thus has repressed this "witch," allowing the complex to absorb more and more of her energy.

Progressively, Vivian came to understand that she must surrender to those aspects of the archetype that scared her so much. Under the shining appearance of Mrs. X, she was running out of libido; she felt lonely and in despair. At the beginning of the analysis, she experienced her "mask" as a jail in which she felt compelled to carry on playing the role of the strong woman—in her work, toward her friends and toward herself. Later, during prolonged work with symbolic materials, she gradually took off her elegant clothes: more concretely, she managed to retrieve some of her projections of shadow onto her boyfriend and parents. She allowed herself to despair and to cry, to get angry; she was less concerned to be perfect and less ambitious in her work.

Of course, such a process does not take place in a linear manner and it involves a lot of suffering. But the pain has initiatic value. Vivian changed, even physically; she was no longer the young, shining *puella,* she had matured. Furthermore, her menstrual cycle returned to normal.

Her case clearly shows how it is sometimes necessary to accept that the only energies potentially capable of bringing about a modification of the situation are dark, negative and seemingly destructive. Vivian's unconscious chose the image of the witch to symbolize these energies; to her this witch was particularly dangerous. Obviously, she might be related to a (negative) mother complex and to the personal mother, as well as to her own femininity. As a result of Vivian's biography, the witch also contains all the sinister dimensions of life that were so present in her childhood, and from which as a little girl she managed to escape by withdrawing into an imaginary world. But she still is the complex in which all the potentially transforming libido became concentrated. Vivian tried without success to eliminate her or to find a more positive figure who could take her place (Mrs. X). Still, the rejected shadow is the archetypal figure that has given her a chance to express her whole personality.

Myths in which the hero must marry an old hag may be used to amplify this motif. In the Arthurian legend, for example, the hero, Gawain, agrees to marry an ugly old woman in order to serve the king. He kisses the hag and she becomes a beautiful young girl—but only during the night, until he allows her to choose when she herself wants to be beautiful.[49] This old hag is akin to the chthonian goddesses of ancient religions such as Kali, the Hindu Goddess: during the rituals in her honor, human sacrifice was required; but she could also inspire creativity. Kali is very close to the dark pole of the Self, containing tremendous energies that can be both destructive and creative. In Celtic literature, and in the Arthurian legend, the hero must discover the "right" attitude toward her destructive powers: by respecting her independence, he frees her, and she in turn will free him.

On the other hand, in German the word *Hexe* (witch) comes from *Hecke* (hedge). The witch is thus "the one who rides across the hedge"; she is in between two worlds and makes communication between them possible. She allows a mutual fecundation and thus contributes to their transformation. She frees psychic energies and helps reorientate them. This applies to the masculine psyche (for which the problem is that of developing a positive relationship to the anima), but it also applies to the feminine psyche, as the above case shows. To my mind, it would be wrong to see the witch only as symbolizing the negative mother who has to be left or fought against. On the contrary, the witch often symbolizes a compensatory attitude which the psyche requires in order to free itself from the behavioral mechanisms and one-sided ego choices that have contributed to a blockage of libido.[50]

Confronting the dark goddess and accepting her also constitutes a form of initiation whose function is to help the psyche effect the passage into adulthood. For instance, in order to survive a particularly traumatic child-

---

[49] See "Sir Gawain and the Lady Ragnell," in Ethel J. Phelps, *The Maid of the North and Other Folktale Heroines.* (The complete story also appears in Polly Young-Eisendrath, *Hags and Heroes: A Feminist Approach to Jungian Psychotherapy with Couples.*)

[50] See Ann Ulanov, "The Witch Archetype."

hood, Vivian had repressed the shadow aspects of life and her own personality. This had allowed her to eliminate at least part of the pain and terror involved and to develop a relatively stable ego. But it had also blocked her development and left her paralyzed in a phase which did not correspond to her biological age; nor had it brought her genuine relief.

Lucifer on Earth

I shall get you, Lucifer, I shall triumph over your nefarious powers! You think that you may do as you please . . . You have destroyed my world, everywhere, always . . . My cosmos . . . And you are now settling in people's hearts, making them as heavy as stones . . . The planets, my planets, my galaxies . . . You have even invaded my black holes, you have taken everything over . . . The sun has spots, the world is rotten, it has been eaten away from the roots . . . Everything stinks, no one can breathe. The children have damn all to laugh about . . . The lakes are radioactive, everything is barren . . . Man is not alive any longer. Look at your children's despair . . . But don't believe for one moment that you have won, I shall fight you, I shall conquer the cosmos back from you. Sin and evil have invaded everything, man has lost hope, people have sacrificed to the golden calf   . . . Look at them, look at their eyes . . . But I shall not let you get away with it. I shall fight you to the bitter end, I shall take my planet back . . . .

During the whole time of the above tirade (of which this is only a fragment), the man delivering it kept his head turned toward the sun. He was shouting, his eyes wide open, standing at the front of a bus in the center of the city, wearing a Napoleon field hat. A heavy silence had invaded the bus; the passengers listened with thoughtful looks on their faces. One man got angry, and mumbled something about "useless people." But, as our crusader was getting out, an old lady turned to me and said: "You know, it is sad, but he is right . . ."

I quote this cosmic delirium because of its expressiveness. Is there a better image of the fight between life and death or of the advent of the "reign of the Antichrist" to which Jung alluded? Of course, one may object that this man was a visionary, a madman, an extreme case. I am not sure whether he really identified with God or whether, on the contrary, he was going to fight alone and conquer the cosmos.

The attitude of the crusader, one who is determined to vanquish evil at all costs, is grounded in the hero archetype and more particularly in its concretization as the pure, fearless knight. The negative pole of the hero archetype is imaged in the rebel. Patrick, an analysand, is one of these rebels, a dark hero who often invests as much energy in destruction as the visionary does in attempting to rescue the world. The rebel's mode is sinister, aggressive, desperate; but, from the point of view of the amount of libido invested, he is a mirror image of his gallant brother.

As a child, Patrick had been the black sheep of a bourgeois family; too often, he had also played the role of scapegoat. His artistic nature, his talent for painting and writing, did not fit in with his parents' academic ambitions for their children. They spent a great deal of time and energy trying to "convert" him. But the more pressure they put on him, by comparing him to his better behaved and more successful brothers, the more Patrick defied them. Yet, underneath his bravado he felt lonely and tearful, a marginal figure in his own family. As a reaction, he gradually developed a violent hatred toward his parents and kept trying to provoke and hurt them.

Vicious circles, of course, and a case that is far more complex than this brief summary would indicate. What is clear is that, contrary to the previous analysands, Patrick never managed to develop a stable ego. His parents' disapproval, which on the surface he sneered at, had been deeply hurtful. He was a sensitive child and easily hurt. By the time he reached adolescence, he was convinced that no one could love him for who he was and that he would have to buy love by doing what others asked of him—which he refused to do.

Thus, instead of adapting to the demands of others, real or imagined, Patrick began a career in anarchy. He projected onto society as a whole his parents' "nastiness" and decided to take revenge. During the following years he was involved in a series of misdemeanors, violent demonstrations and grandiose provocations; he spent some time in jail and later lived as a drop-out with other marginal people. At that time, he went through a very deep crisis and attempted suicide, almost succeeding. But, paradoxically, his rebellion contributed to giving him a degree of stability: "alone against all others," he felt strong and his rage carried him.

During all these years, Patrick kept painting in an autodidactic manner, finding relief in his art. He sold a first picture almost by chance, and gradually gained a reputation as an artist. A gallery organized exhibitions of his work and he made some money. His attitude toward this success was ambivalent: the fact that his art was valued by others gave him more self-confidence, but he was convinced that no one really understood his message. This message may be summarized in one sentence: "Just look and see how rotten the world is!" Patrick paints end-of-the-world landscapes, dark desperate scenes, full of haunted, persecuted creatures. He says he wants to "shake people up," to "draw them away from their little bourgeois, blind happiness"—which he unconsciously envies.

In the course of the analysis, the depression Patrick had managed to transform into aggression slowly emerged. His dreams were a continuous series of brutal scenes, catastrophes and deaths. The violent figures of his paintings followed and attacked the ego. The ego normally managed to defend itself, but it could never quite get rid of its attackers. Patrick's aggressiveness, which manifested among other things in a need always to dominate and control others (and brought various relationships with women to an end), was in fact an expression of a total feeling of helplessness toward the nefarious fate that seemed to keep destroying his life. It was also an expression of a deep feeling of being a victim of the "radioactivity" and the "sterility" he projected onto the world and that could attack him at any time in the shape of a disease: Patrick is a hypochondriac.

Every time he feels threatened by a situation or by a person, Patrick becomes terribly aggressive. But the aggression that he channels into his art leaves him totally helpless. The pictures are a direct cry from the unconscious, and while he is working he is totally flooded, almost in a trance; and as soon as a painting is finished, he panics. He then gets into his car and drives for hundreds of miles, without a specific aim—another way of running away from depression.

Our long analytic relationship was characterized by a progressive passage from aggression to depression: during a first phase, Patrick's despair erupted in the form of violent tirades directed at me and at the analysis. When a number of chance events precipitated a crisis by shaking his precarious balance, the sessions became the container in which he could let go and safely express his despair. He discovered that he need not panic when violent forces attacked him. He let his depression get the better of him and learned that in time a less threatening phase would come. During that period he also talked about his paintings; this gave him some distance from them, and he was better able to work actively on them.

In any case, for Patrick the analysis was aimed more at learning to cope than at working on symbolic material. He refused to talk about his dreams and was not interested in trying to discover their meaning. Simply bringing them into the *temenos* of my office seemed to somewhat depotentiate their threatening energies. The analytic process took place purely on an emotional level. By sharing with me his emotional reactions to the threatening power expressed in his drawings and deep depression, he gradually learned that he could live despite his despair. The analysis did not cure his depressions—and I don't think he expected it to—but it did help him come to terms with them.

As a result of this kind of process, another passage has taken place. Patrick has stopped running away from a fate he experienced as incredibly dark; he feels more responsible for his own destiny, for his own life. Instead of being only a victim, he has become an actor, and this allows him hope.

I shall say more later about the importance of hope in analysis.[51] Suffice it to note here that it was hope that impelled Patrick to find an analyst, and later to keep coming to the sessions, despite the fact that, through them, the depression he had been stubbornly avoiding was brought to the surface. The feeling that something was happening, even if not a cure in the traditional sense, led him to give up his plan of committing suicide. He says, almost with sarcasm, that his hope is nothing but an illusion, a chimera, since tomorrow will be no better than today. But he also believes that if he gave up hope, he would simply die.

At a deeper, more emotional level, Patrick's hope is genuinely alive. It was well expressed at the very beginning of our work in a dream image that became very precious to him. In the dream he was on a raft floating in between deep, black straits; there was a storm and icy rain was falling. The raft was caught in turbulence and he had trouble not being thrown into the water. But in the distance, where the river flowed, he could see a lake with a small fishing harbor on its shore.

This was the first dream with a positive tone to it that Patrick could ever remember having.

The Center of the World

Neither the bus-riding visionary nor any of the analysands described above identified completely with the negative forces in their life. Each in their way tried either to compensate them or to stop them from being too threatening. But what happens when a person becomes progressively convinced that there is no chance to win? What does one do when, without identifying entirely with the destructive pole, one loses the distance necessary to react? We may think here of suicides where the individual self-destructs out of a conviction that all is lost anyway, that is, stops fighting before

---

[51] See below, chap. 6, espec. pp. 122ff.

being destroyed. It is, then, a kind of flight forward: death (whose death?) was going to triumph in the end; it might as well do so immediately.

Jung writes that normally compensation serves as a kind of self-regulation of the psychic system, but in certain cases—particularly where there is a latent psychosis—it may lead to suicide: the destructive tendencies flood consciousness, taking possession of it.[52] He carefully avoids any comment on the meaning of such a death, and, of course, the problem of suicide is not an easy one. I do not intend a detailed discussion here, but suicide is one possible reaction of the psyche to the domination of the negative pole of the Self and that is why I mention it. The ego identifies with the destructive forces and turns against itself.

One may object that suicide is sometimes justified, and that in certain cases the person's decision must be accepted. Indeed, often the suffering involved is so great that no one should be asked to bear with it. Those who consider that everyone has a right to suicide, that is, a right over their own life, are in fact granting absolute freedom to the ego. According to them, the individual, conscious ego has a logical and irrevocable right to decide and to act. However, when the ego is flooded by unconscious destructive energies, the idea of free choice is an illusion. With other suicides, the decision may be more conscious, more deliberate. But in each case, the ego stops being a relative component of the Self. It is no longer able to dialogue with a transcendent dimension and is not being carried by it. To speak more broadly, the ego may believe that it can control the Self, when it may in fact be disposing of it. The ego decides—or thinks it does. Do we know what happens to the Self in such a case? Or can we be sure that the Self wanted the death chosen by the ego?

James Hillman, on the other hand, argues that a death instinct is being ritualized in suicide. According to him, the analyst's task is to be objective toward the phenomena of the soul, "taking the events as they come without prior judgment," and must never adopt an "attitude of prevention" toward suicide.[53] It is also useless to try and explain suicide through the use of psychological concepts. One must understand the archetypal, mythical meaning of the analysand's actions. In this sense, the impulse to death may be interpreted as an impulse to life, "a demand for a fuller life through the death experience." Symbolically speaking, the suicidal choice "asks

---

[52] "On the Nature of Dreams," *The Structure and Dynamics of the Psyche,* CW 8, par. 547.
[53] *Suicide and the Soul,* p. 48.

directly for the death experience." Hillman concludes that "until we can say no to life, we have not really said yes to it."[54] Death—brought closer through the suicide attempt—thus opens a way for transformation; from the point of view of the psyche, death is not an end.[55]

My own view is that when one manages actually to dispose of oneself, no one can tell whether a transformation has really taken place. Too many suicides are "accidents": a sudden impulse, a cry for help, a moment of panic, but the person is found too late or manages to inflict fatal wounds. And I wonder whether, in those cases, another choice might have been possible, a choice that would not leave a corpse behind. Hillman looks at suicide symbolically and mythically, an approach that raises far too many questions to be adequately dealt with here. One would at least need to effect a distinction between the different forms of suicide and their causes—such as the wish for self-destruction, rage and a need for revenge, feelings of helplessness and an attempt at exerting power over others, ritual sacrifice and the frustrated need for mirroring.

A somewhat different form of the flight forward is found in some romantic literature, particular German, where death is fondly aspired to. There, death itself becomes the nourishing mother, whereas the rational contemporary philosophical discourse on suicide tends to take palliative action against the lack of nourishment by, first, overemphasizing and then annihilating the orphan ego. Other writers (for instance Novalis, Thomas Mann) aspire to a symbiosis with the mother, with death, so that she can free them from all suffering. In psychological terms, the ego, trapped in a sinister inner world, aspires to a fusion with the Self in order to forget the terrors of everyday life.

I am thinking of an analysand, a woman in her forties, who was obsessed with the wish to die. Her deep depression and her absolute lack of energy actually prevented her from acting this out. But she was an addict and would combine tranquillizers and alcohol to keep herself in a paradisiac state of near-death and, thus, in contact with the powers beyond her control. I think, too, of a patient in a psychiatric hospital who kept describing in detail how he would die soon. He gave me precise instructions as to how to bury him and how his grave should look. He felt he would start living only when he was dead and that his grave should be a witness to this

---

[54] Ibid., p. 63-64.
[55] Ibid., p. 66.

fact. His daily life was pure torture and he had decided not to take part in it any longer: he was waiting for the "true life," in which he could embrace the world which was really his, that of the collective unconscious.

It does seem that, in some cases, psychosis represents an attempt to return to the original Self, the Self as it was before the ego (inadequately, unilaterally) detached itself. It looks as if some patients instinctively try to find the unity, the nourishment they are deprived of in their everyday life, by fusing with a Self that is more complete than the one they are experiencing; that is, by returning to a sacred time in which everything is still possible, they may be able to build a more stable ego-Self axis. Very concretely, the above patient refused to eat, saying he would be fed by the mysterious powers that awaited him in the Great Beyond; death itself had become his source of nourishment.

Let us now look at the case of Mary, an analysand who at one point in her life has, in the terms used by Hillman, "said no to life, in order to really say yes to it." The discussion of her case will allow us to understand more clearly the consequences of an experience—voluntary or not—that touches upon the roots of being itself. Can those who "reemerge out of their craze and into their so-called normal ego"[56] forget their vision and adapt to a normal life?

Mary, a woman in her thirties, has terrifying memories of her adolescence. At the beginning of our work, she gave me a few details on what she called her "madness." After having been a quiet, dreamy child, she came into contact with drugs as a teenager, trying out different substances without becoming addicted. One day an LSD trip turned bad and she went through a psychotic episode during which she suffered third degree burns to her hands—she had put them directly on the burner of an electric stove, having seen the "center of the world" behind the red-hot plate. The psychosis lasted for a few days, with hallucinations. She was hospitalized in a state clinic and remained there for almost a year. During this time, she was very suicidal and made a number of attempts that she now describes as being more the expression of "nostalgia for another world" than a genuine will to be finished with life.

When she came out of the hospital, Mary managed to reintegrate into society to a surprising degree. She received professional training, married, had two children. Only her husband knew of her "madness," and others

---

[56] See quoted passage from Perry, *The Far Side of Madness,* above, p. 20.

would probably have been very surprised had they heard about it. She says that her psychotic experience gave her a "great inner strength" that allowed her to overcome several very difficult times due to family tragedies. She tried to lead a "more-than-normal" life and was determined to forget the episode that had marked her adolescence. For about fifteen years she succeeded. But then, almost out of the blue, she began feeling very depressed; she also had sudden violent suicidal impulses. She described these as "a sudden longing for death, like the craving for a drug, almost physical," without any outer event provoking them. Mary managed not to act out these impulses and they would disappear after a few hours. But she was terrified by the idea that they might be a sign that she was becoming psychotic again.

A number of her dreams clearly reflect her problem. For instance:

> A number of people are eating at the dining room table, as my guests. Vincent, who is sitting on my left, goes into a kind of delirious speech about the meaning of life and of the planets. Dr. Z is sitting at the other end of the table, on the right, and is commenting on Vincent's ideas in a patient but slightly irritated tone: she is trying to say they do not make sense. He goes on talking and she promises him he will feel much better after he has taken the medication she wants to give him. I go to the kitchen to get the dessert. It is strawberries with whipped cream. The old cook tells me to prepare Vincent's and Dr. Z's dessert and shows me how to do it. I spend a lot of time washing and then cutting the strawberries in such a way that both will have exactly equal shares.

Vincent was a patient who was hospitalized with Mary. He represents the dark, psychotic side of her personality. She was very young at the time of her psychosis and was not really able to deal with what had happened. She says she has kept memories of moments of abysmal terror which at the time she wanted only to forget. She had had a good relationship with Vincent, who suffered from schizophrenia, but she also remembers being scared of him. Still, he remained a fascinating figure to her, the one who "knew" instinctively about the deep meaning of life. Dr. Z had been her physician in the hospital.

In the dream, Mary at first spontaneously takes sides with Vincent, reflecting the fascination she had unconsciously repressed after the powerful experience of her psychosis. The old cook, a chthonian woman (but also the one who knows how to use the red-hot burner at the center of the world without getting hurt), shows her how to feed Vincent and the doctor simultaneously, giving them equal shares. The strawberries are a beautiful and common symbol of libido and of Eros.

Consciously, Mary identified with the physician, the one who had helped her back to a normal life. But Dr. Z is also the one who treats and eliminates symptoms by giving tranquilizers. Mary has put to sleep the Vincent side of her personality, the side that is in fact the most productive and the most lively. Her depression, at least in part, comes from a feeling of emptiness, a lack of existential intensity compared to what she had experienced during her psychosis.

Jung, referring to similar cases, writes of a "regressive restoration of the persona": after unconscious contents have brought the ego into chaos, or even caused it to collapse, individuals may react by adopting a narrow personality and the mentality of a scared child, living below their potential; that is, they restore their persona in a regressive way.[57] They then live as they would have before the crucial experience, not only ignoring what it has taught, but also hesitating to attempt things that would be within their ability. They thus lead a shrunken, unsatisfactory life.

Mary recovered fully after her psychosis and even learned to use the experience as a source of inner strength. But the dreamy little girl, full of fantasy, had become a reasonable woman who had overadapted to collective norms; she had chosen to be unilaterally healthy for fear of going back to "madness." The unconscious thus reminds her of "Vincent's" existence, in the dream but also in the form of suicidal impulses that, in her case, must be understood as expressing a nostalgia for the state of fusion with the Self that she had experienced during psychosis.

We may, at another level, formulate a hypothesis that the tragedies she experienced while she was leading a "normal" life represent a series of negative synchronicities, through which the shadow she had lost contact with was concretizing itself. More important, the impact of these tragedies had amplified the questions that had haunted her during her hospitalization and which may be summarized as, "Why me?"

In other words, Mary experienced her psychosis as part of a dark fate that was trying to destroy her life; she thought that, despite all the years of apparent normality, she had had more than her share of problems and trouble and was thus unwilling to accept going back into these. However, it was only after she started confronting the terrifying experience of her psychosis through intensive work on her dreams and other symbolic mate-

---

[57] *Two Essays,* CW 7, pars. 471ff.

rial that it began to acquire meaning and thereby contribute to making her life richer. From that time on, her "Why me?" also found at last a partial answer. The energy trapped in the complex was freed and she started to reorientate her life with great enthusiasm. At the time, a dream confirmed that she had found the right attitude:

> A woman, all dressed in black, like a widow, is lying on the ground; she is twisting and turning, her arms are hitting the ground as if she was possessed. The other onlookers are very scared and want to give her an injection. I go to her and take her into my arms. She doesn't resist and immediately calms down. Her face is beautiful, peaceful. I feel good.

Paradoxically, the suicidal impulses that haunted Mary resulted in fact from a concrete partial suicide. She had stopped herself from living fully by repressing the traits represented by Vincent. Her unconscious was, in a way, mourning her own death. One may of course easily understand her misgivings, remembering the frightening experience of her adolescence. For her, it was truly a matter of, in Hillman's words, "asking directly for the death experience" in order to be able to live again.

A widespread motif that served to amplify one of Mary's dreams (in which someone was forbidding her to take part in her own funeral) was helpful during this period of our work: that of "the king who did not want to die," and so made a pact with the Devil in exchange for eternal life.

Simone de Beauvoir, in *All Men Are Mortal,* gives this a different twist: a man is *condemned* to live eternally. Over the centuries he loses all capacity for seeing, tasting, laughing or crying, seeking and being surprised. Everything becomes boring, monot-onous; he loses everything that made up his personality, even his capacity to be moved by emotions. He knows that he has no possibility of experiencing anything new, that the same events will repeat themselves for many centuries to come. Therefore he is unable to love since, for him, love will only repeat itself many times and be boring. He ends up envying mortal people, longing in vain to join the humanity from which he is cut off.

Through her "partial suicide," Mary had unwittingly put herself in a similar situation. She had to accept dying again and to allow herself to bury the "king," the physician who eliminates pain rather than understand it, or in other words the persona that protected her from confronting her inner Vincent.

The question "Why me?" is one that may not always be answered as clearly as in Mary's case. I am thinking, for instance, of those suffering from endogenous depression or even, to some extent, of Patrick, whose life has remained a daily struggle; I am also thinking of those who were not as lucky as Mary and remained prisoners of psychosis. These are tragic fates; their only meaning, as I have said, may be to show others a different perception of reality and of the shadow realm.

To end this series of examples from practice, I would like to mention an image from a dream a client brought me while I was writing chapter two of this book, "God's shadow," a fact he was not aware of.

> A castle on a hill, a rather large building. Flags are floating in the wind. One of these looks like a beautiful and mysterious standard: in its upper half, there is a huge black cross on a sky-blue background; below is a devil's head, fire red and yellow, on a light green background.

The analysand was fascinated by this motif, because he could not connect it to anything he had met so far in his dreams. He drew a picture and brought it to the next session. The flag is a square standing on one corner, a horizontal line divides it into two triangles. The blackness and shape of the cross stand in sharp contrast with the burning face of the devil. The two triangles (the blue at the top, the green at the bottom) are not clearly separated, with the colors almost running into each other.

At the beginning of the analysis, this man had had to learn to surrender an extremely controlled attitude toward his life in order to contact the shadow aspects that had dominated it. He commented: "The cross is that of Christianity . . . but in the dream it had a threatening aspect, not as it should be with the Church. And, as I was painting the devil, I kept trying to make him look dangerous and evil. But the more I tried, the less it worked out." (His devil does have a shrewd, malicious look, but even so it does not suggest anything evil or threatening.)

This dream came at a time when nothing had happened in the man's life that could be seen as having provoked it. It seems to me that its images come from a deeper level of the unconscious, from collective, archetypal strata. The motifs introduced in the next chapter belong to the same category.

5

Archetypal Schemas

According to Jung, the confrontation with the Self in its light and dark aspects follows a more or less constant archetypal schema, which he defines as individuation. Throughout different epochs and different cultures, humanity has attempted to express this schema in the symbolism of myth and ritual. Many of these delineate, implicitly or explicitly, a passage through the sequence of death-transformation-rebirth. But the course of this process may vary, and myths or rituals can either focus on specific aspects or illustrate a more global evolution. It can also express a chain of transformations, which Jung specifically means by "the individuation process."

The motif that Jung calls the night sea journey occurs frequently;[58] an obvious example is the Biblical story of Jonah in the whale. As shown there, the individual must go through a regression into the "mother's womb," in order to return from the journey with a greater degree of consciousness and a more mature attitude toward the chaos of the Self. In other words, a maturation process, away from symbiosis with the original Self and the mother, must take place.

Implicit in many myths of this type is the idea of a heroic journey: the hero symbolizes the ego voluntarily confronting the darkness, the depths of the unconscious. Of course the hero meets with threatening, dangerous events; the search seldom follows a linear course and he makes mistakes, becomes dispirited or comes close to giving up. But the hero is frequently guided by positive figures who provide the strength to carry on. The quest is eventually successful and the hero is transformed—or, rather, the situation that precipitated the journey is transformed.

It is usually quite adequate to interpret these myths this way. In certain cases, this interpretation is the only possible one. But as far as our theme is concerned, the image of the triumphant hero is not the only useful one. In other words, this image is incomplete, for it does not always suffice when confronting the unfathomable or sinister aspects of the Self. To be sure, the hero needs to be strong and brave enough to overcome obstacles. One chooses to undertake a journey, perhaps moved by an impulse that is not

---

[58] See *Symbols of Transformation,* CW 5, pars. 538f.

fully conscious, but actively participating in the search. Psychologically speaking, this presupposes an ego stable enough to focus on a given aim and grounded enough not to be destroyed at the first difficulty.

Not everyone has such an ego. Besides, a less heroic, less active attitude might prove just as useful. Then the aim would not be to triumph over obstacles in order to reach a fundamentally new, transformed situation, but rather to best use the limited energy at the ego's disposal to find a new kind of grounding. This would allow for renewal from within, with strength and hope coming from an intrapsychic flow of energy.

In that sense, the propitious attitude needs not always be heroic, and it is not always ego-consciousness that must be broadened. With respect to the individuation process, a new form of awareness may be more important for the analysand than reaching a specific aim—or even than a Logos-type understanding of the way the psyche functions. In order to show what I mean, I shall examine a myth that illustrates a heroic quest, but I shall view it from a different angle.

The Grail and the Hero

The basic Western motif of the search for the Grail, that is, for a mysterious treasure, is found in folktales of the type exemplified by Grimm's "The Devil with the Three Golden Hairs." Here is a summary:

> A youth who has been born under a lucky star must go to hell to bring three hairs from the devil's beard. On his way he is asked various questions to which he must find the answers (for instance why a tree does not flourish; when a ferryman will be freed of his duties; how the sick prince or princess can be cured; why a spring has gone dry). He gets help from the devil's mother or grandmother and receives the three hairs; he also learns from them the answers to the questions. On the homeward journey he answers the questions and receives a large reward. The king attempts to imitate his exploits and dies; the hero marries the princess.[59]

In the Grail legend proper—a Christian legend that rests at least partially on historical facts and of which there exist many different versions—these motifs are organized in the following way:

> A mysterious, life-preserving and substance-dispensing vessel (the Grail) is guarded by a king (who does not want to die) in a castle that is difficult to find. The king is either lame or sick and the surrounding country is devas-

---

[59] *The Complete Grimm's Fairy Tales,* no. 29, pp. 151ff.; Aarne and Thompson, *Types of the Folktale,* types 461 and 461A.

tated. The king can only be restored to health if a knight of conspicuous excellence finds the castle and at the first sight of what he sees there asks a certain question ("Whom does the Grail serve?"). Should he neglect to put this question, then everything will remain as before; the castle will vanish and the knight will have to set out once more upon the search. Should he finally succeed, after much wandering and many adventures, in finding the Grail castle again, and should he then ask the question, the king will be restored to health, the land will begin to grow green, and the hero will become the guardian of the Grail from that time on.[60]

The best known among many versions are those by Chrétien de Troyes and Wolfram von Eschenbach. De Troyes' *Perceval* belongs to the Breton Cycle and was completed after his death by various authors. Von Eschenbach's *Parzifal* remains close to de Troyes' but supplements it with an ethical and religious perspective on chivalry. It has a more serious, less imaginative tone and asks the questions of the nature of good and evil and of the responsibility of man toward God. In this version, the Grail is not only a mysterious, fascinating object; it becomes a symbol of inner life and of ascetic discipline. Parzifal seeks extreme spiritual purity, and his Grail is not a vessel but a stone. This version may thus be interpreted in its relation to alchemy, as a compensating movement to the Christianity of that time. Jung has shown that alchemy had attempted to fill the gaps left open by the tension characteristic of the twelfth and thirteenth centuries. But let us go back to our basic version.

Here, the Grail is a relatively well-defined symbol: it is said to be the cup from which Christ ate and drank and instituted the Eucharist on the day of the Last Supper. In another version it is the cup in which Joseph of Arimathea received the blood of Christ at the Descent from the Cross. Joseph founded a community whose members met every day around a table, in honor of the Grail. They kept a chair free for its future defender.

Jung interprets the vessel as a feminine symbol and comments on the need for medieval Christendom to renew itself through the inclusion of feminine and irrational aspects.[61] At another level, the Grail vessel with its bivalent contents (the Eucharist *and* the Crucifixion) may symbolize the Self, including its nourishing and death-bringing aspects, that is, life and renewal versus pain and despair. It also symbolizes that part of the Self we may never grasp, God's immanence as manifested through symbols.

---

[60] Summarized from Emma Jung and Marie-Louise von Franz, *The Grail Legend.*
[61] See *Psychological Types,* CW 6, par. 407.

In the Christian legend, and in von Eschenbach's version in particular, the quest becomes an allegory for the continuing search for God, for the God-image. Within this context, the Grail vessel may be connected to the sacred vase or even to the magical cauldron of Celtic mythology, the provider of ever-renewed nourishment.[62] It is also akin to the alchemical cauldron. As a mythological vessel it dispenses life and healing, strength and wisdom; it may contribute to a transformation similar to that taking place during the Communion mystery of the Mass. As a hidden treasure, it may be found where the grass is greenest, where a meteorite has fallen, or at the end of a rainbow, which connects it with a cosmic dimension. More generally, the Grail can be seen as the provider and container of soul substance; it may image the transcendent function and may contain the capacity for psychic synthesis between conscious and unconscious. Its discovery allows one to live in harmony with oneself, and to be nourished by the Self—precisely the qualities the ailing king is lacking.

In fact, in many versions of the legend there are two kings, whom the Celtic tale calls the Fisher King and the Old King. It is obvious that the two royal figures represent different aspects of the same psyche, but the distinction between the Fisher King and the Old King allows for a more precise interpretation. For my own purposes, and in order to simplify, I shall follow only the hero's path and try to understand what Perceval or the future Grail King represents, without taking account of the different figures he meets on his way—not even that of Gawain, with whom he makes up a classical pair of twins, or light and dark brothers, such as are found for instance in the Gilgamesh-Enkidu pair. I do not look into his origins either (in one French version, the hero is Galahad, son of the knight Lancelot). For Chrétien de Troyes, who remains closer to the popular version of the legend, he is simply a young man who has lost his father and has been brought up by his mother. He discovers that he is interested in chivalry and goes to King Arthur's court.

The original situation corresponds to that of an individual who is wounded, has lost any sense of meaning, and who does not feel alive any longer (the barren country or waste land). The Fisher King—the ego, the dominant attitude of consciousness—is not capable of healing himself; libido is blocked. The Old King, the Grail's keeper, is sick too; unable to die, he cannot effect the passage to the next stage of life. The problem,

---

[62] Ibid., par. 401, note 149.

then, is twofold: the Grail cannot feed either the Fisher King or the Old King. Both life and death are blocked, neither passage can be traveled.

The problem results from there being too great a distance, or a lack of communication, between the opposites, between conscious and unconscious. The hero's task, at least initially, will be to reestablish the flow of communication and libido. Put in terms of the Self, the Fisher King is near the life pole, but he cannot be fed by this life; the Old King is close to the dark pole—the unconscious and death—but he cannot confront them and the vessel he guards is of no help. Neither king can help the other. Also, in his role as the keeper of the treasure, the Old King plays the same role as the devil in the Grimm tale.

In terms of individual psychology, this type of situation results from a one-sided consciousness, whatever that may be: the ego may take too rational a position and repress the irrational, or it may focus on the material aspects of life and neglect the spiritual, or it may have chosen good to the exclusion of evil, etc. There is a lack of wholeness; inherent aspects have been excluded from the totality of the Self. In this polarization, the Fisher King and the Old King cannot contact each other.

At the time when the Grail legend was written—the beginning of the thirteenth century—the suppressed elements may have been connected mainly to the feminine, chthonic dimensions of life: both the Christian and chivalrous ideals stress other values—courage, purity, the light aspects of Eros. The tale of "The Devil with the Three Golden Hairs" was probably produced by a similar collective situation, since it is the Devil's mother, or grandmother, who, symbolizing natural wisdom, helps the hero find the answers to the riddles. In both cases, there is a split between the opposites, and the Grail vessel may symbolize the alchemical cauldron in which these opposites can undergo a chemical reaction and mutually transform.

As we have seen, initially the Fisher King cannot truly live and the Old King is unable to die. Both consciousness and the unconscious need renewal. Their sterile relation needs to be modified, and the individual's attitude toward them must be transformed. In Jung's terms, the transcendent function must be constellated in order to reconnect the ego with both the positive and the negative poles of the Self. It is this healing task that the Fisher King delegates to Perceval.

Who, then, is Perceval? How does he relate to the transcendent function? How will he be able, by embracing both poles, to reconnect them and to free the libido that was blocked?

It is said that he is a knight, but a number of versions also call him a fool—not a madman, but a youth who is a bit childish and innocent. One could of course blame him for lacking the maturity he may need to be the true hero who has to grow away from the unconscious and from the mother, toward a broadened consciousness. But I also see Perceval as the fool in a more positive sense. He is the one who does not follow a straight path, who surrenders the security of a rational, one-sided attitude. He is close both to an active instinct and to sublimation, but also to blind impulses and to the unconscious. In some versions these two aspects are in fact attributed to two figures, Perceval and Gawain, who represent two poles of the same archetype. Furthermore, the fool touches both on the divine and on the animal nature of man and so can reach beyond that paradox. His spontaneity is not destroyed by the tension between opposites, and so he can follow every path, without being determined by reason and collective norms. This is precisely what enables him to overcome the split, that is, to heal it.

The fool belongs to the realm of Eros, in both its dark and light aspects; he obeys feeling and the irrational. Obviously, before he can leave on his quest Perceval must be conscious enough to accept the challenge and determined enough to set out for his goal. He cannot be an unconscious fool, but fool he must be, needing sufficient innocence (the child's innocence in a positive sense) to remain in contact with the worlds of the spirit and of the instincts, with both the active ego and blind impulses from the unconscious. From the beginning of the quest, the presence of Perceval the fool justifies the hope that the initial situation may be transformed, that a vital element will unblock the flow of libido.

Leaving aside the various stages of the quest, I stress only those aspects important for my purpose. Perceval, like the heroes of so many tales, makes mistakes, often does not know where the path is taking him, sometimes has to retrace his steps and at times gives up. But as a fool, he instinctively knows that the shortest way is not always the best, and that quite often a *circumambulatio* will bring him closer to his unseen aim than a head-on approach. This aspect too is connected with the instinctive wisdom of Eros as opposed to the purposefulness of Logos: the path with heart is not as linear as logic and reason; it includes shadows and apparent failures. To follow it requires patience and the surrender of absolutes.

However, and this is very important, Eros is neither sterile nor aimless; it involves an investment of vital energy, real work. I am reminded here of the ritual work discussed in chapter three, where the participants actively allow the sacred chaos to irrupt into the linearity of profane time. Whenever the hero, or the initiate, is "foolish" enough to submit to these energies, a renewal can take place. Obviously, passive submission does not suffice to effect change; work is required, together with an openness that allows the participants to be touched at an emotional level. Perceval accomplishes this ritual work by persevering on his path and not being discouraged by his mistakes or dispirited by obstacles. Because he manages to stand the chaos and even to be inspired by it, his unflinching exertion takes him further. Because Perceval shows heart, that is courage and the ability to forego measuring himself against a model, he finally succeeds and finds the Grail castle.

At a more schematic level, we could formulate the steps of this quest as: a) separation from the old (wounded) attitude, b) letting go under the guidance of the fool and c) being able to assimilate the new elements, each of these steps involving an investment of energy. This schema requires neither linearity nor a need for all the steps to be successful. In fact, for a psyche that finds itself in the initial situation described above, it does not matter much whether the quest actually succeeds, that is, whether the Grail is found or the question answered. This is shown by the fact that, as soon as our hero asks the "right question" and before he actually gets an answer, the country is regenerated and both kings are healed.

Thus I see the quest itself as being far more important than its results or its aim. The psyche in which the fool is present, through Eros and the unflinching will to be under way, inevitably generates the vitality missing when both kings were sick and the poles of the Self were split. To my mind, in the case of Perceval but also of numerous other heroes, any interpretation that insists on linear steps and the definition of precise aims denies the quest its truly healing dimension. Psychologically speaking, even when apparently nothing is being achieved, energies are flowing and effecting a transformation.

In the Grail legend, Perceval finds the Old King's castle and asks the crucial question. He then succeeds both kings, which means transformation takes place at both conscious and unconscious levels. In other words, the hero finds his place in both worlds, sacred and profane. But the question he asks, as well as the answer he is given, are not the clear ones demanded by interpretations of the hero that stress Logos and the search for absolute truth. He asks: "Whom does the Grail serve?" and the answer is,

"The king." The question, first, is somewhat paradoxical: Perceval was sent on his quest specifically to find a cure for the disease suffered by the Fisher King and his kingdom. The answer thus seems redundant and becomes less mysterious only if we remember that the Old King, despite being the keeper of the Grail, cannot be nourished by it, being blocked in a hopeless situation. The "king" to whom the Grail may belong, then, is likely to be a new king symbolizing an attitude in which polarity is transcended, a king who can relate to both of its poles.

I do not insist on this formulation, although some versions of the legend, and an interpretation according to which it reflects problems in medieval Christendom suggest specific answers. But it seems to me that if the quest is taken as a search for a mystical center, for a God who would correspond to the true nature of the Self, it is quite natural that the legend's question and answer could only be formulated through a paradox. In this they are put in a way that is adequate to the true nature of the Self. If too much stress is put on meaning, the problem of the dark side of God is not solved. In the legend, it is neither spiritual nourishment nor sublimation that make it possible to reconnect light and darkness and to heal the king's wound. It is an innocent question, asked by a fool carried by Eros, that brings new life.

Further, it is not—at least in certain versions—a pure, fearless knight endowed with a high degree of spiritual perfection who finds the Grail. It is a human, in his fool aspect, who by accepting the chthonic and the irrational and by learning to use a new form of thinking—an alchemical turn of mind—asks the question that will eventually transform the situation.

Of the analysands presented in the previous chapter, it is of course Miguel whose quest eventually most closely resembled Perceval's. I mentioned that at the beginning he was highly motivated and sincerely sought healing. But he was trapped in his ideals and tended to move at too rational, too heroic a level.

For instance, after he started sliding into the abyss of isolation and loss of reality, all the attempts I made at depotentiating a situation that I considered dangerous brought no result: Miguel objected that he would get nowhere unless he was totally involved. Not that he wanted to remain on the edge of psychosis, but he took no account of my warnings—motivated, as I now see, by my own fear that this stage would come to a bad end. In this sense Miguel showed heart, but he remained for too long the fearless knight; and in insisting on marching on no matter what was happening, he did take a risk. Also, it was only after he progressively allowed himself to be guided by a more foolish type of hero that he found renewed vitality.

The traits I have emphasized here are found in numerous other myths and folktales. For instance, there are tales in which a naive or even dumb hero commits one mistake after the other, where animals—the instinctive dimension of the fool—know the way and help the quest to progress, or where the development of Eros, through a confrontation with both the other sex and with the anima fulfills this function. But I would emphasize one thing above all. When interpreting myths related to individuation, that is to the relation with the Self, one should take full account of the manner in which a patient acceptance of sinister aspects brings the hero further.

Analyses in the traditional heroic mold are prejudiced toward light and a positive attitude. In a way, they proceed in too rational a manner. And they may forget to ask the right question, that is, to integrate an acausal dimension that is inherent to the nature of the soul; in looking for A, we may find B, and this B is precisely what the psyche may need.

In the tale recounted at the beginning of this chapter, the Devil himself is present and guards the treasure. Only because that hero succeeds in relating to the grandmother—a witch who eventually assumes a positive role —does he find the answers. The adequate attitude there, the hero's way of confronting the dragon, does not involve cutting its head off.

Initiatic Surrender

One aspect of the confrontation with God's shadow is not sufficiently shown by the examples given so far: that of absolute, unadulterated despair or, rather, the concrete, physical experience of the morbid and threatening dimensions of the Self.

Of course, Perceval and the heroes of numerous other tales go through times of doubt, are afraid or lose hope. But I am interested in that precise moment when the hero or heroine gets to a point where it seems everything is really lost and nothing at all can ever happen. The hero, then, is plunged into a feeling of absolute helplessness or, more dramatically, discovers the existence of destructive forces that cannot be controlled.

I shall look into this dimension by introducing an initiation ritual and a myth. It is also found in many fairy tales, expressed by motifs such as that of the protagonist being exiled or jailed (for instance at the top of a tower, as in Grimm's "Rapunzel")[63] or wandering for many years (looking for a

---

[63] Cf. Aarne and Thompson, *Types of the Folktale,* type 310.

lost relative or a future husband),[64] or having to wear rags or an animal skin for months or even years.[65] In each of these tales, the focus is on the long wait and despair in a situation that seems hopeless.

I have chosen to present somewhat more dramatic examples, in which ascetism—and pain, but this is not the most important aspect—stands in the foreground. In these, the final means of passing to the next stage are provided by a nonheroic, submissive attitude where the sufferer persists in spite of an apparent lack of reason to hope. Here, psychic progression is not brought by pain as such, in the sense of a price to be paid, but by surrendering to an apparently hopeless situation. It is not by coincidence that my examples—the initiation of an Iglulik shaman through the contemplation of his own skeleton, and the descent to the Netherworld of Inanna, the Sumerian goddess—come from societies whose gods and goddesses were close to nature, and who promote an attitude nearer to the feminine and chthonic than to the active purposefulness of the masculine.[66]

Among the Iglulik Eskimos living near Hudson Bay, the shaman is responsible for relations with all the supernatural powers that may influence everyday life and survival.[67] He thus plays an essential role in many different domains, that of hunting for example, but also in healing, since disease may result either from not respecting a taboo (such as violating the prohibition against certain foods), or from the patient's soul having been stolen by a dead person. One becomes a shaman on the basis of an individual vocation, and the shaman does not occupy an official position within the group, as he does for instance in Siberia. In Eskimo tradition, anyone may practice as a shaman after having gone through an apprenticeship with a master.

In the most important stage of the apprenticeship, the actual "making" of the shaman, the novice spends many weeks or months isolated from the group, in a desolate place where he expects to meet the animals that later

---

[64] Ibid., type 451 (e.g., Grimm's "The Seven Ravens").

[65] Ibid., types 510, 510A and 510B (e.g., Perrault's "Peau d'Ane," Grimm's "Cap o' Rushes").

[66] As almost everywhere else here, "feminine" and "masculine" are meant in a broad, schematic sense. An exclusive classification of psychic elements as to feminine or to masculine runs contrary to Jung's fundamental reflection on the "bisexuality" of the psyche; but whenever abstract schemas are formulated, the contrast feminine-masculine cannot be entirely avoided.

[67] The description of shamanic rituals that follows is based on my reading of, among others, M. Eliade, *Shamanism: Archaic Techniques of Ecstasy,* and E. Holtveld, *Eskimo Shamanism.*

will be his helping spirits. Quite often he suffers concretely, physically, from the cold and hunger.[68]

He also has to learn to see himself as a skeleton and to denominate each of his bones in a ritual language. Until he reaches this stage he remains alone in the cold, without any food; he just rubs two stones together until he sees himself as being robbed of his clothes and even of his flesh. He then goes on a journey under the sea to visit Takánakapsâluk, Mother of the Seals. This journey will be repeated during the sessions held to ask for an abundant hunt. He also takes another (flying) journey to the Great Beyond, during which he gets to know his auxiliary spirits. But the essential stage is that of the illumination, during which, after having been reduced to his own skeleton and having learned the name of each of his bones, the novice will get to know his life soul.

The Igluliks have two souls, a life soul and a name soul, of which only the life soul is eternal. A parallel with the Jungian concepts of ego and Self does not seem far-fetched, insofar as the Self, by serving as a bridge to the collective unconscious, is in contact with the *illud tempus,* initial time and the whole man. By coming in contact with the life soul the novice builds a relationship with a transcendent dimension; the rubbing of the stones, taken as symbols for the two souls, images how this is achieved. The stones could also be seen to symbolize the two poles of the Self.

Generally speaking, the stone is a symbol of the Self because its hardness partially exempts it from decay. It is thus the antithesis of life forms subject to the laws of change and death. The stone is also a symbol of cohesion and of the harmonious reconciliation of different aspects of oneself.[69] In alchemy the Philosophers' Stone symbolizes the conjunction, or coming together, of the opposites—psychologically, the integration of the conscious Self with its unconscious side; here again, the dynamic of rubbing against each other, ego and Self, name soul and life soul.

Let us go back to the ritual and the process involved. With regard to the practice of analysis, I would like to stress two aspects: the importance of the preparation phase and the fact that the novice is unable to influence the duration of the initiation.

By being isolated from the group, the novice leaves everyday life, its norms and its security. A space is created in which another way of living

---

[68] For ease of reading here I use masculine pronouns, but women may also apprentice to become shamans.

[69] Cirlot, *Dictionary of Symbols,* p. 299.

can be learned. One's teachers are animals, creatures that stand closer to nature and to the unconscious. In other words, before experiencing illumination, the novice must return to a more basic existential level, closer to the roots of being and the collective unconscious.

This aspect is of course present in any ritual and roughly corresponds to van Gennep's separation phase. In chapter two, I focused on the importance of the liminal phase. I now wish to stress that this phase cannot be reached without adequate preparation. To fully participate in the analytic process, the ego must be aware, so to speak, of leaving everyday life, of moving to another space. I have observed, and encouraged, a tendency in analysands to open (and also to close) sessions by making a specific gesture or saying particular words. I think that, on a very small scale, this is an equivalent to the separation phase. The ritual shaping of sessions can of course also be interpreted as an attempt, by analysand or analyst or both, to create continuity and an analytic vessel that feels secure because it has a degree of predictability. But I believe that the other aspect is—must—also be present: in order to be open to what might happen in the liminal phase, one must first leave everyday life and prepare oneself. This may happen more or less unconsciously and be expressed symbolically, but only after this step has been taken is the ego, the novice, ready for the next phase.

I see the period of waiting that follows as being already part of the liminal phase, since the novice's gestures are no longer those of everyday life. With regard to analysis it shows an essential dimension: illumination can only come spontaneously, when the psyche is ready. It will not come if the space hasn't been made, but also it will only come when the time is ripe, psychically speaking. The rubbing of the stones symbolizes this patient waiting which, I think, must be learned as much by the analyst as by the analysand. The soul has its own rhythm and we cannot do much to accelerate it—tempting as at times it may be to intervene so that the analysand may not have to go through what is generally a difficult phase.

The Iglulik type of initiation takes a less dramatic form than that of, for example, Siberian shamans. The Eskimo novice is not as brutally dismembered as the Siberian one, and the initiation often omits a violent death followed by a resurrection; its contents are more sublimated. The experience is symbolic, imaginary. It is typical of the Iglulik novice that physical asceticism and mental contemplation bring him to a state of near-death in which he patiently rubs his stones until achieving illumination. Analytic processes that take a similar form are not necessarily easier to accompany than those in which there is more obvious suffering. But again, the novice's initiation shows how relative the ego (and its impatience) is and, in a sense, how relative suffering may be. Once he has seen his skeleton the Iglulik will return to everyday life with a different attitude.

The symbolism of the skeleton is found in numerous cultures, where the bone is the ultimate source of life, since the soul resides in the skeleton. In Jewish tradition, bone is an indestructible, corporeal particle, symbolizing the belief in resurrection.[70] By contemplating his own skeleton, the Iglulik novice experiences his fundamental being, his absolute nudity as a human, together with the dark, death aspect of life. He literally finds his soul, as an autonomous reality independent of the short life of his ego. He reaches this stage by going through ascetic loneliness and physical pain, but without being dismembered and practically annihilated as is his Siberian counterpart. But the lesson is the same: compared to the transpersonal dimension, the ego world is relative.

The myth of Inanna's descent to the Underworld includes physical death more directly, as well as a motif close to the dismemberment of the Siberian novice. I will examine only these parts of the myth, although Inanna's entire story could also be interpreted as a confrontation with shadow aspects and the integration of the dark pole of the Self. Here is a summary of the myth as told by Sylvia Brinton Perera:

> At the first gate to the Netherworld, Inanna is stopped and asked to declare herself. The gatekeeper informs Ereshkigal [Inanna's sister], the Queen of the Great Below, that Inanna, "Queen of Heaven, of the Place where the sun rises," asks for admission to the "land of no return" to witness the funeral of Gugalanna, husband of Ereshkigal. Ereshkigal becomes furious, and insists that the upper-world goddess be treated according to the laws and rites for anyone entering her kingdom—that she be brought "naked and bowed low."
>
> The gatekeeper follows his orders. He removes one piece of Inanna's magnificent regalia at each of the seven gates. "Crouched and stripped bare," as the Sumerians were laid in the grave, Inanna is judged by the seven judges. Ereshkigal later kills her. Her corpse is hung on a peg, where it turns into a side of green, rotting meat. After three days, when Inanna fails to return, her assistant Ninshubur sets in motion her instructions [to look for her].[71]

Inanna is eventually freed, but not without having to find a substitute who will take her place in the Underworld for part of each year.

---

[70] Ibid., p. 29.
[71] See *Descent to the Goddess: A Way of Initiation for Women*, pp. 9-10.

Here, the initiation happens progressively: a shining, triumphant goddess loses her attributes, one after the other, surrendering all her privileges and facing the death inflicted by a sister living in the land of no return. Later, she has no alternative but to rot, impaled on a stake and entirely dependent on others for her liberation.

Ereshkigal, Queen of the Great Below, represents neglected, repressed aspects of the Self and the power in its negative forces. The myth describes her as a pitiless figure, prone to terrifying fits of rage; her husband's death has plunged into a mourning of cosmic dimensions that annihilates everything around her. Inanna has known only the opposite pole, ruling in light and wealth. She must now experience what it means to be robbed of everything one loves. Her apprenticeship culminates in the time during which her body rots away on a stake and she is absolutely deprived of everything that made her a queen. In order to become this queen again, she will have to compromise, striking a contract with Ereshkigal to share her life during part of the year.

The parallels between Inanna's experience and shamanistic dismemberment are fairly clear. On the other hand, the myth is more concrete, less sublimated than the initiation rite, and this makes its narrative more impressive and more frightening. Inanna truly suffers, in body and mind, at the hands of the dark Self; she is almost entirely destroyed, putrefied by shadowy powers.

Before relating this to the propitious psychological attitude, let us note that Perera focuses her interpretation of the myth on its relevance for women. In my approach, the initiation taught by Inanna is valid regardless of one's gender. One may claim that for both men and women the anima serves as a guide to the unconscious; it is also the anima who knows when surrender is required. But I do not like using this type of feminine/masculine model. We may at most consider that, archetypally, the elements required for an initiation through surrender—unconscious, patient, irrational traits—have always tended to be associated with the feminine realm. The myth of Inanna's descent fits into this trend. But there exist other myths in which the figures are masculine—think of Orpheus and Osiris, for instance, or even of Christ's descent to Hell before his Resurrection—without the symbolical message being fundamentally different.

Does the discovery of a propitious attitude toward the nefarious aspects of the Self necessarily require ego-destruction and putrefaction? I have chosen this myth as an example because I believe it does. But I wish to caution against erroneous conclusions as to the actual psychological mechanisms involved. Where physical death and dismemberment actually take place, one may be too quick to apply the schema of death-transformation-resurrection, thus wrongly interpreting suffering and even death as a sine qua non for transformation. Psychic death and dismemberment may need to take place, but they do so because they are an integral part of life and not as a price paid for wisdom and new life.

I see this distinction as essential, insofar as the schema death-transformation-resurrection is too often interpreted as implying a bargain or exchange. In that perspective, pain would ensure transformation and death would almost automatically bring renewed vitality. To my mind, it is just as valid to see the experiences of death and suffering as necessary, but only because they are part of life and because there can be no real vitality without the tension resulting from the inclusion of the dark pole. The myth of Inanna clearly shows this: she will have to spend so many months of each year in the Netherworld.

As for the shaman—whether Eskimo or Siberian—he experiences the coexistence of life *and* death during his initiation, learning that they belong to the fundamental nature of being and the Self. This is what will allow him to grasp the essential dimension of being, and thereby to reenter profane life so as to help his tribe survive.[72]

In terms of the value of initiatic surrender, the means for confronting the pain involved in shamanistic apprenticeship is anything but heroic: the shaman has only his patience and the slow rubbing of two simple stones.

---

[72] In courses and workshops organized nowadays, shamans are often characterized as "the wise ones," people who have risen above their tribe after going through an initiation process that allowed them to "know themselves." However, studies of tribal life show that shamans went through the ritual *for* the tribe, using their gift for the benefit of the group and not in order to become someone special; further, the idea of individuality had little place in these cultures. Through their initiation, shamans learned to confront dangerous forces and to survive them; but when they were not holding a seance, they were normal members of the tribe.

I mention this because I have heard analysts being equated with shamans and some complaints about the isolation accompanying individuation. In my experience, work with the individual psyche leads to a more meaningful involvement with the collective. Individuation takes place in settings other than analysis, and those who have developed an adequate relationship to the Self feel strongly that they have a place in the human group: in Jung's words, they have become "equal to all." (See above, p. 54) This has nothing to do with isolation. As for analysts, or therapists of any kind, the feeling that one "knows more" can only lead to an inflationary identification with the healer archetype.

Inanna has nothing at all and depends on her assistant for help. In both cases, and even more so in the second one, the confrontation is not active and cannot be entirely conscious. Time and a ritual framework, or the help of others, will determine the outcome.

Put in the psychological terms of the actual analytic process, I believe that the function of the analyst is to accompany the analysand through this form of initiation and to accept its reality. The confrontation with the negative pole of the Self necessarily implies a certain amount of patience and suffering. The analyst's role cannot be to help the analysand avoid pain. One can accompany the process and, by trusting in the Self, help constellating in the analysand the hope that, even after long periods in hell, despair will not be the whole of life. However, this will happen only if the tension between light and dark, hope and despair, has been kept for long enough to bring about a renewal in the flow of libido.

Because our society insists on positive and positivist attitudes, it is necessary to stress a fundamental truth: only if they are kept together and related to properly can the two poles of the Self ground life in a healthy manner. This also applies to analysands who do not have a stable and flexible enough ego. In precisely their case, the experience of great suffering has remained sterile, not leading them any further. They may suffer from an inner feeling of emptiness or they may be mourning for the abandoned child; they suffer from not being sufficiently grounded to let themselves be carried by the flow of life, or they may ache from being tormented by an obsession with shadows. For them, it is an improvement if that suffering can be awarded a function and integrated into a vital line.

As stated earlier, my aim is to formulate with more precision the components of the propitious attitude. Besides an acceptance of pain, they involve, as shown by the examples given, patience and the ability to persevere, a capacity for making oneself as small as possible, for accepting passivity—but not indifference—until the difficult times are over; submitting to an instinct that suggests apparently absurd gestures (for instance the rubbing of the stones); trusting that assistants will be there, and realizing that, despite feelings of deep despair, some routine, commonplace and nondramatic actions will help keep the ego outside the kingdom of shadows. And finally, a certain asceticism is required, an acceptance of things just as they are and renunciation of the need to explain and control.

A parallel comes to mind, from traditional peasant cultures that face the forces of nature without modern technology. In the peasant's attitude, the seasons have their own rhythm and will. Cosmic forces that are both nourishing and destructive determine whether the harvest will be abundant or totally ruined.

This picture also reveals another important dimension: the peasant accepts the presence of negative forces, rather than identifying with or being fascinated by pain and destruction and thereby risking inflation. Analytic work always involves the risk of inflation and this tendency may lead the analysand into a fascination with the negative. Natural and psychic forces *are* both nefarious and destructive. They are also terribly powerful, in the sense that, despite being negative, they contain tremendous energy. In order to be useful, confrontation with them must include respect for the dangers involved. In other words, one has to keep enough distance from them not to be destroyed, while coming close enough to be touched, without much illusion that it will be possible to triumph. The peasant does just this, and so does the Iglulik novice, patiently rubbing his stones.

Vivian, referred to in chapter four, needed to allow herself to experience her inner chaos and despair; she also needed to initiate a dialogue with the witch or dark goddess who, from her unconscious, was absorbing so much of her energy. One of the many paintings she did in the course of her analysis represents this goddess as a Medusa from whose head snakes are rising. The Gorgon Medusa was capable of turning into stone whoever looked at her. This shows how justified was Vivian's fear of the forces she had repressed.

On the other hand, she was very afraid of losing her friends, including her companion, if she expressed the dark goddess's rage. The analysis thus became a very gradual process, during which work on dreams and pictures was slowly transferred to a more everyday level. Vivian progressively abandoned her royal attributes, that is, her concern with perfection and control, and learned to accept anger and despair. She was able to effect this change with sufficient awareness of the process, in other words with an active enough ego participation, so as to avoid being totally overwhelmed or "rotting away on a stake." But she often had to rely fully on her capacity to endure pain and to be patient before she was able to go forward on her own path, leaving behind the hell of this transitional phase.

The Innocent

In order to outline the archetypal foundation of some of the points discussed above, I turn now to another tale. Perceval, Cap o' Rushes or Cinderella, Inanna and even the peasant living close to nature or the Eskimo novice rubbing his stones, are guided by a complete Self, by an instinctive knowledge of what is right. In folktales, the type of hero that best corresponds to this archetype—that of the divine child, as we shall see—is the innocent or dummling who makes one mistake after the other, but eventually brings back the treasure or marries the king's daughter, whereas his more clever brothers come back empty-handed. It often looks as if everything is happening *against* him and *for* the other figures, but by following his instinct he paradoxically makes his way.

I have chosen a tale in which this motif occurs in its most elementary form, "Hans in Luck."[73] Here is a summary:

> After working seven years for a master, Hans decides to go back home. He receives as wages a piece of gold "as big as his head." He gets under way, carrying the gold on his shoulder. After some time, he meets a rider on a smart horse, who tells him he will trade his horse for the gold. Hans is very tired of carrying the gold and he accepts. The horse starts trotting and throws our hero off the saddle; it would have run off had not a peasant who was passing with his cow held him back. Hans complains about the horse's vigor and agrees to trade it for the cow. He is delighted, as he is thinking of the milk, of the butter and cheese that he will be eating. As he walks further, it gets very hot and he feels tired and thirsty. But when he tries to milk the cow, he receives an enormous blow from one of her hooves and faints. When he comes round, a butcher gives him a drink and tells him that his cow will never give milk because it is far too old. Hans agrees to trade the cow for a pig and, later the pig for the goose offered by a young boy.
>
> As he arrives in a village with his goose, he sees a sharpener with his grindstone. He tells him his story and the sharpener convinces him that he should practice the same trade, so as to always have enough money. Hans gives the sharpener his goose and takes the grindstone. He goes on his way, but the stone is heavy and he is tired. He puts it down on the edge of a fountain while he is drinking and the stone falls into the water. Hans thanks the Lord for having delivered him of a heavy burden and walks on, empty handed, on his way home to his mother.

Although other tales of this type use different motifs, they all follow the same schema: the hero enters foolish bargains and trades what he owns for objects of lesser value, each time pleased at having made such a good deal. In this Grimm version, Hans is delighted, for instance, at not having to walk any longer (the horse), having enough to drink and to eat (the cow),

---

[73] *Complete Grimm's Fairy Tales,* no. 83, pp. 381ff.; cf. Aarne and Thompson, *Types of the Folktale,* type 1415.

having meat (the pig), feathers for his pillow (the goose) and enough money (thanks to the grindstone). And, after he has lost everything, he is pleased at being rid of his burden. The tale ends with these sentences:

> "There is no man under the sun so fortunate as I," he cried out. With a light heart and free from every burden he now ran on until he was with his mother at home.

We might readily apply this tale to our materialistic society. But I have chosen to interpret it with regard to the archetype of the divine child. The image of the stone slowly grinding, monotonously, seems to echo the eternal dimension of this child and the passage of time which, in other narratives, is symbolized by the motif of the spinning woman, whose fingers guide the threads of destiny.

With every new bargain, Hans is delighted that he has received exactly what he needs and feels blessed by fate. He does not take account of the intrinsic value of the objects or animals, but values their usefulness in relation to their concrete potential in his current situation. His instinct tells him that each bargain is "right," and he does not care whether a collective system of norms would see things differently. According to these norms, his bargains are, of course, foolish: he is a naive character who is constantly being cheated. But his naivety does not prevent him from making his way home, from reaching the place where he can be himself.

I do not see the tale as ending with a negative regression, even though Hans returns to his mother (in another version, he goes home to his wife and wins a wager when his wife does not get angry at his having lost everything). Rather it would seem that, by progressively surrendering material possessions or, more precisely, by discovering the potential in what he has at the time, he gets closer to a situation in which he will be in harmony with, and nourished by, the Self.

The tale obviously introduces negative experiences in a rather mild way; that is, the apparent value of the objects keeps diminishing. However, if we try to imagine what the situation of some analysands would be after these successive losses, we can easily feel their anguish and maybe their rage: less grounded in the unconscious than Hans, they would inevitably feel that a dark fate keeps trying to destroy them, by progressively depriving them of possessions they value. Whereas our hero's trusting attitude toward fate, together with his conviction that what is happening to him cannot be entirely negative, place him within the realms of both the positive pole of the Self and the divine child archetype.

According to Jung, this archetype has different aspects:

> It is a striking paradox in all child myths that the "child" is on the one hand delivered helpless into the power of terrible enemies and in continual danger of extinction, while on the other he possesses powers far exceeding those of ordinary humanity. . . . The "child" is born out of the womb of the unconscious, begotten out of the depths of human nature, or rather, out of living Nature herself. It is a personification of vital forces quite outside the limited range of our conscious mind; of ways and possibilities of which our one-sided conscious mind knows nothing; a wholeness which embraces the very depths of Nature.[74]

The above passage comes from a section titled "The Invincibility of the Child." The notion of invincibility must be understood in a restrictive sense, for the divine child does not acquire powers by conquering evil, but because its nature is such that it goes beyond evil by including it. The archetype in all its numinosity implies the tremendous and the unfathomable, whereas the reality in which Lucky Hans lives is much simpler. But since he is being guided by the divine child, he is in contact with the essence of nature, his instincts and a totality that transcends him.

This transcendent dimension is described by Jung:

> The "child" is therefore *renatus in novam infantiam*. It is thus both beginning and end, an initial and a terminal creature. The initial creature existed before man was, and the terminal creature will be when man is not. Psychologically speaking, this means that the "child" symbolizes the pre-conscious and the post-conscious essence of man. His pre-conscious essence is the unconscious state of earliest childhood; his post-conscious essence is an anticipation by analogy of life after death. In this idea the all-embracing nature of psychic wholeness is expressed. . . . Wholeness, empirically speaking, is therefore of immeasurable extent, older and younger than consciousness and enfolding it in time and space. This is no speculation, but an immediate psychic experience.[75]

At this level, one may say that the child "knows"; contact with archetypal energy and instinctive wisdom allows the child to reconcile conscious and unconscious forces, to keep in touch with both light and darkness. Like the Self, the child is the most adequate representation of the vitality that can potentially overcome death by integrating it. The child's instinctive simplicity is the source of a strength greater than that of the hero.

---

[74] "The Psychology of the Child Archetype," *The Archetypes and the Collective Unconscious,* CW 9i, par. 289.

[75] Ibid., par. 299.

"Smaller than small yet bigger than big,"[76] the child can overcome darkness, unify, create, recreate and save.

The divine child archetype may not be too far remote from that of the fool; affinities certainly connect them, in that, for instance, both know how to move in the world of instincts. But I see Lucky Hans as being endowed with a talent that Perceval probably lacked: he is able to transform a negative situation since, by relating it to powers that transcend it, he is able to give its contents, both positive and negative, a place within a dimension that goes far beyond consciousness. Within the divine child, the light and dark poles are so close to each other that, as soon as one is constellated, so is the other. Perceval and Cap o' Rushes followed an instinct that allowed them to cope with a given, temporary situation; for Hans, each situation just *is,* each stage of his journey having an intrinsic value.

Of course, the conscious attitude symbolized by Perceval and Lucky Hans can be present only in an individual who feels sufficiently contained in a fecund cosmos and who is able to trust in destiny, despite obstacles or misfortune. In other words, it requires a positive mother complex, a secure background. Many analysands suffer precisely because they lack this positive grounding. Yet even when this dimension is lacking or difficult to contact, I believe that the analyst needs to keep in mind the importance of a childlike attitude, or risk not nurturing certain potentials for transformation. Contact with the fool and the child may be established through the unconscious, both in the symbolic material and in the transference-countertransference relationship. An awareness of its importance implies, at least on the part of the analyst, an open, almost naive belief that anything is possible and that irrational elements play an essential role. This approach balances a more pessimistic, less flexible conscious attitude. And finally, awareness of the fool or child reminds us that appearances may deceive and that the negativism present in the foreground may hide deeper values that are waiting for the propitious time to become concrete.

One may object that I am not being very logical: having stressed from the beginning the importance of a confrontation with the dark pole of the Self, and having considered healing to result not just from a constellation of the positive, I have now introduced the images of the Grail Quest and Lucky Hans as underlining rather positive, healthy elements. However, both the archetype of the fool and that of the divine child are characterized

---

[76] Ibid., par. 283.

by their containing *both* poles of the Self without the ego having to effect choices. The fool does not ask too many questions and simply accepts that the extremes of light and dark can be simultaneously present. He does not reunite the opposites but attributes equal importance to them. There is thus a strong tension, but this does not prevent the fool from acting on impulse, without taking account of collective values. The divine child *is* the opposites, holding both poles within, extremely close to one another.

The foregoing may explain why, as soon as these two archetypes are constellated, the psyche is better able to confront the negative without dichotomization or repression.

What is more, the analyst's task is also to help the analysand connect with a more complete Self, which requires more than a simple compensation of the dark side of the psyche; a journey is needed into the negative aspects at an archetypal level. The archetypes of the fool and the divine child allow this passage. As components on which the propitious attitude may be grounded, they lead the analysand along an axis that includes hope. As for the novice, Inanna and, as we shall see, Christ at Gethsemane, they are closer to an axis modulated by despair and may thus teach the analysand how to accept this despair. They may also help compensate the need for perfection that so many clients manifest: trapped as they are in a normative system that keeps asking for achievement, happiness and objective progress, they tend to transfer to the analysis the conviction that others (including the analyst) will love them only if they are happy or achieve something. The notions of surrender to despair, initiatic passivity and acceptance of the dark pole may contribute to an evolution of this attitude. They may also help the analysand avoid resignation.

To return to the divine child, a further distinction seems useful: that between a childish attitude and a childlike outlook on psychic reality. To encourage the first in an analysand could create dependencies and provoke sterile regressions. To develop the second involves giving the right place to the child within the adult psyche without rendering the individual helpless. The mother, the "good enough mother" of D.W. Winnicott, does not invest herself completely in her child, nor seek to prolong the childhood period. She gives the child a chance to develop and to leave her, while keeping enough innocence to rely on more than conscious rationality. It is only then that the individual will be able to rely on being secure within a nourishing archetypal mother, and to trust a transcendent dimension.

The case of Patrick discussed in chapter four seems, at first, a bad example of a quest in which the archetype of the divine child played an essential role, at least compared to the way it manifests in the tale of Lucky Hans. In Patrick's inner process, the constellation of this archetype must be understood as a compensation. His ego, drowned in negative tendencies and haunted by dreams in which one child after the other was being harmed, could only rely on the power of a divine child to counterbalance the situation.

Psychologically speaking, the more the ego loses the battle against the attacks from the negative pole of the Self, the more urgent it becomes that it should accept it rather than try to escape and, especially, that it remain in close contact with the Self. The divine child symbolizes a complete Self at a very early stage and its constellation serves as a bridge to this Self. In Patrick's case, this constellation remained entirely unspoken during the sessions—as the analytic dimension of the whole process was in any case. But it manifested in emotional interactions, in body language, and in images which served to support the process.

Once Patrick had surrendered to regression and depression, other unconscious forces were mobilized and he was gradually able to feel safer. He is, of course, still far from trusting life, but he has discovered that losses do not always imply a disaster. He has acquired an underlying feeling of being part of the human group and has developed a solidarity toward at least some segments of this group. It may have been the fact that, during the whole time of his rebellion and aggressive behavior, his attitude remained one based purely on emotion and instinct—as opposed for instance to a rationally critical stance—which made it possible for the analysis to intervene. Accordingly, the tone of his emotions has changed and he no longer perceives his own life in destructive terms only.

Gethsemane

I hesitated before choosing the motif of Christ in the Garden of Gethsemane; its interpretation may well be beyond the means of a nontheologian. But it is one of the images that accompany me in my work and I would like to reflect briefly on the message it contains for me.

> Then he said to them [the disciples], "My soul is very sorrowful, even to death; remain here and watch with me." And going a little farther he fell on his face and prayed: "My Father, if it be possible, let this cup pass from me; nevertheless, not as I will, but as Thou wilt." And he came to the disciples and found them sleeping; and he said to Peter: "So, could you not watch with me one hour? Watch and pray, that you may not enter into temptation;

the spirit indeed is willing, but the flesh is weak." Again, for the second time, he went away and prayed, "My Father, if this cannot pass unless I drink it, Thy will be done." And again he came and found them sleeping, for their eyes were heavy. So, leaving them again, he went away and prayed for the third time, saying the same words.[77]

"Thy will be done," but the underlying question is also, "Does Thy will have to be this?" Jesus knows what awaits him, and knowing his Father's will his soul is ready to die with sorrow. He is alone with the terror of his coming Passion and death (in the French version of the Gospel it says: "Father, if it is possible let me escape this awful death awaiting me"). If the Father demands the Son's death, how can he be a loving God? God suddenly makes Jesus understand that Lucifer, evil and death are not only man's work, but that He Himself takes part in their power. The Devil becomes part of God and there seems to be no choice for Jesus but to accept this. Jesus asks God whether there is an alternative, whether he must drink this cup. However it is not with the Father that he seeks to share the anguish in his soul, but with his disciples, his human companions who are asleep—and so he must remain alone with his dismay. And he knows that there would be no escape from temptation if he avoided confronting his fears alone, for he might be seduced by the hope that there could be a less painful way.

He is also tempted to finish with it, there and then. He is tempted to accept death from a "good" Father in Gethsemane, rather than the death on the cross imposed on him by a "bad" Father. Could he be delivered from the awesome realization that his Father is not only good and loving? And yet, if God's will is to be respected, then evil must have its way. Jesus' despair is provoked by an inescapable perception: God's will, which he always obeyed until now, is akin to the powers of evil that he has resisted, that he wanted to resist under all circumstances. He tries three times to avoid accepting this; three times he tries to question the ineluctability of the alliance between the Father and evil. And, three times, he accepts it. "God has drawn a pact with death and he is about to sign it."[78]

If, as Jung says, "Christ is our nearest analogy of the Self and its meaning,"[79] then the man Jesus in Gethsemane symbolizes the situation of the

---

[77] Matt. 26: 38-44, Revised Standard Version.

[78] K. Barth, *Die kirchliche Dogmatik IV—Die Lehre der Versöhnung,* teil 1 [Church Dogmatics, vol. 4—Doctrine of Reconciliation, part 1], p. 298.

[79] See above, p. 27.

ego confronted with the totality of the Self. It is by accepting death on the cross that Jesus will make it possible for his disciples to believe in his resurrection. And it is this belief that will make him a symbol of the Self, for from then on he will be "the Christ." But in Gethsemane Jesus is human, only too human. It will only be from the moment when this human being accepts the opposites, when Jesus submits to a Father whom he now sees as both benevolent and hostile, that the *imago dei* will be incarnated.

In this sense, the image of the Crucifixion may also be seen as an illustration of what the ego experiences when it has to accept the Self as not being only positive. Because the ego constantly assigns values, because it can only perceive in terms of opposites such as good/evil, life/death, it can be torn and it will despair. Indeed, it will only be when the ego—Jesus—realizes that the Self—God—is simultaneously both poles of each pair that it can find a solid grounding in its own fate. After this decisive moment, the symbol incarnated by the Christ changes: it is more adequately related to a Self in which good and evil *just are,* without the rending of Gethsemane. It is also only after Jesus accepts the Father's malevolent intentions as part of their relationship that this relationship can be one of genuine understanding. It is within this type of understanding that the ego can free itself from moral values and find a place in the cosmos.

The idea of evil is produced by consciousness; it implies an evaluation through the ego. At the level of the Self, the sinister aspects, that is, the negative pole, are of course dark, but they do not imply a moral notion of evil or destruction. In Gethsemane the negative pole is also death, as the Self demands that the ego step back. But the immediate death that briefly tempts Jesus would not be the death that would allow the Self to fulfill its function. Whenever the ego longs for this kind of termination, so as to be delivered from the fundamental conflict that Jesus must confront in Gethsemane, it effects a false sacrifice: it is prepared to give up life so as not to be forced to accept that life is also death. I believe that this type of sacrifice may well be at the root of certain suicides.

It is obvious that acceptance, as such, requires, a sacrifice. How can we believe in a God who, apparently, does not love us and who is not only good? How could Abraham believe in a God who demanded that he kill Isaac? How can we accept surrendering the hope promised by a loving God? In fact, our spontaneous tendency to see God as loving may lead us to a false understanding of the sacrifice required. In the case of Gethsemane, a resurrection will of course eventually take place; but it would be wrong to see it as planned by a God who, after all, was only loving. On a psychological level, we may think that since confronting the negative pole gives the individual a feeling of vitality and allows him to become more human, everything is not as dark as it may have looked. But to my mind it would be wrong to see the resurrection as implying that the Self is only benevolent; the Self, or God, is only an entity in which the opposites co-incide—or, from the ego's point of view, even conflict.

If it is very difficult to avoid falling into this type of thinking, it is even more difficult to formulate the problem. However, I believe that it is important, psychologically, to understand that finding the propitious attitude toward the Self does not imply believing that, in the end, good will win and evil will lose. The confrontation with the Self does not open an optimistic perspective on life. But it does allow a peace of mind, based on the simple experience that if both poles are assigned their proper place then neither will gain the upper hand—this peace is symbolized by the point at which the two arms of the cross meet. It also makes it possible to surrender a constant need for control and security. It is this need, expressed in various hierarchies at the ego level that, by eliminating the paradoxes of the relationship between the ego and the Self, may well lead the confrontation to a bad end.

Let us go back to the analogy between God and the Self and to the despair in Gethsemane, in order to formulate more precisely the paradox. For the ego—Christ in His human nature—the only possibility of feeling close to a "complete God"—to the Self—is to accept this God's shadow aspects, Lucifer and the Crucifixion. Or, in other words: if God, and the Self, are to keep their truly divine nature, if they are to transcend and nourish, then they must have wholeness and thus be malevolent too. Jesus must accept Satan in God, because otherwise this god would not be God. What is more, for Christ this acceptance will also involve a passage through hell, before the Resurrection.

This motif, together with that of the cross, is very much akin to that of Inanna's descent to the Netherworld and her putrefaction on a stake. Yet there is a difference between what I have called "initiatic surrender" and the phase of "despair in Gethsemane," since the first is more passive than the second. In analysis, initiatic surrender allows the individual to bear a painful experience of the dark pole and establish contact with transpersonal forces that may provide a broader context for personal despair. This involves a rather passive acceptance of the situation, in which the ego discovers means of surviving it. The despair in Gethsemane, on the other hand, demands a more active ego participation, in which it must surrender control and its hope of a positive fate.

My experience with analysands has shown me that this is the hardest step to take. Quite often it is preceded by a long phase of deep depression which may be all the harder to accept because it comes after the ego had started emerging from a previous feeling of hopelessness. It is as if the psyche is now destroying all hope that the difficult phase was just that, a phase, and that it can be overcome. During the despair in Gethsemane, the unconscious is in fact saying that the negative will remain present in the individual's life. What is more, in this phase it must be integrated into everyday experience; the dark must have its own place in the analysand's cosmos. I am reminded of the *aggrégation* phase of the rites of passage: what has been experienced during the liminal experience must be woven into everyday life. The novice is no longer the same person, either in sociological terms or in personal terms.

On the other hand, the idea of a liberation through surrender may well be misinterpreted, in the same way as the schema death-transformation-rebirth is sometimes misinterpreted (see above), when it is understood too literally. The ego must renounce its supremacy, and must give up wanting to control every aspect of life or to avoid the suffering implied in accepting the paradoxical nature of the Self. It is not that, by surrendering blindly to the Self in order to be happy, the ego has then simply paid the price of a resurrection. The sacrifice of the ego must be effected with respect for the transcendent nature of the Self.

Jung alludes to this in the following passage, where he writes of the tension between conscious and unconscious:

This [renunciation] can happen in two ways:
1. I renounce my claim in consideration of a general moral principle . . . . In this case the "self" coincides with public opinion and the moral code. . . . It is projected into the environment and therefore remains unconscious as an autonomous factor.
2. I renounce my claim because I feel impelled to do so for painful inner reasons which are not altogether clear to me. These reasons give me no particular moral satisfaction; on the contrary, I even feel some resistance to them. . . . Here the self is integrated; it is withdrawn from projection and has become perceptible as a determining psychic factor.
These two ways of renouncing one's egoistic claim reveal not only a difference of attitude, but also a difference of situation. In the first case the situation need not affect me personally and directly; in the second, the gift

must necessarily be a very personal one which seriously affects the giver and forces him to overcome himself.[80]

Let us apply this to the present discussion: If I accept the shadow of the Self because I think this may allow me to overcome it (in a mechanistic way), then my ego will remain in control. If, on the other hand, I accept it because I have experienced it emotionally as being a part of my life—which I do not necessarily like—then I am related to the Self in a very genuine and personal manner. Simultaneously, by acknowledging that transcendent forces exist and that they may influence my ego world, I give up trying to control every aspect of my life, painful or not. I am "related to the unconscious powers within [me] of life and God [and, I would add, of death]. This is redemption."[81]

This being said, it is obvious that at the concrete, everyday level, no decision can or should be taken without the active participation of the ego. Giving up control does not mean abandoning responsibility.

The "right," fruitful type of relationship between the ego and the Self is clearly shown in the image of Jesus in Gethsemane, seen as a symbol for the best possible attitude toward the *imago dei*. It may also be exemplified with the help of another notion, that of the interdependence between God and man, including the idea of the relative nature of God. This idea is found, for instance, in the texts by Meister Eckhart, a great mystic whom Jung often quotes. For Eckhart, there exists an intimate affinity between man and God, which contrasts very much with the Christian sense of sin and dependence. Eckhart's perception of God and His relationship to man is deeply psychological, and relative in the sense explained by Jung:

> The "relativity of God," as I understand it, denotes a point of view that does not conceive of God as "absolute," i.e., wholly "cut off" from man and existing outside and beyond all human conditions, but as in a certain sense dependent on him; it also implies a reciprocal and essential relation between man and God, whereby man can be understood as a function of God, and God as a psychological function of man. From the empirical standpoint of analytical psychology, the God-image is the symbolic expression of a particular psychic state, or function, which is characterized by its absolute ascendency over the will of the subject, and can therefore bring about or enforce actions and achievements that could never be done by conscious effort. This overpowering impetus to action (so far as the God-function mani-

---

[80] "Transformation Symbolism in the Mass," *Psychology and Religion,* CW 11, pars. 393-395.
[81] See above, p. 55.

fests itself in acts), or this inspiration that transcends conscious understanding, has its source in an accumulation of energy in the unconscious. The accumulated libido activates images lying dormant in the collective unconscious, among them the God-image . . . .

Hence, for our psychology . . . God is not even relative, but a function of the unconscious.[82]

Simplifying, we may say that, psychologically speaking, God and the Self are not external to man or absolute—in which case man could only either submit to them or revolt against them, instead of participating in them. God and man, the Self and the ego, are perceived as interdependent, and find an appropriate meaning or a concrete function only within a mutual relationship. Within the right relation, each finds a true place. This understanding attributes a primacy not only to the soul, that is to both the ego and the Self, but also to their relationship. In a sense, the Self realizes itself through the ego, while the ego can only find its right place within the Self. This, as we may note, also implies that at Gethsemane God *depends* on Jesus: if He is to keep His divine nature, He needs Jesus to accept its totality. In the same way, the Self is dependent on the ego: it is only after the ego accepts the despair provoked by the demands of the Self that the Self may fulfill its true (healing) function.

Psychologically, for me, the image of Christ in Gethsemane symbolizes the crucial moment, the fundamental conflict that an analysand encounters after giving up the compensation mechanisms which had allowed him or her to avoid facing the sinister dimensions of life or to confront negative impulses by identifying with them. This conflict can only be resolved by a genuine acceptance—which, I may add, can never be quite as lasting as it may sound here. Regressions, changing circumstances, ego illusions, a longing for a "better world," may all lead to a periodic reactivation of the conflict. Of course my schematic discussion cannot entirely reflect everyday reality, but I still wish to stress that since nothing is static in the psyche, accepting the dark can only be a long—and often painful—process.

Some of my work with Mary exemplifies this. After she had understood what had made her react in a "regressively adaptive manner," she saw that she would have to confront the "Vincent" side of her personality. This she first refused to accept. She was scared of having to repeat a terrifying experience, but mainly her feeling of "having already had more than her

---

[82] *Psychological Types,* pars. 412-413.

share" reactivated her conviction that God did not love her, since He asked so much of her. She told me that she envied "everyone else"—that is, all those whose fate appeared to have been lighter.

During the years when she had had to face a series of distressful experiences ("negative synchronicities"), Mary had been able to rely on what she had learned during her hospitalization: that dark, fateful times do not necessarily last for ever. Yet, she had not truly accepted that those were also part of herself. Months of intense work were required before her resistance could be overcome. During this period, Mary, like certain other analysands, was blocked by her inability to "overcome the despair of Gethsemane" (and, what is more, often overwhelmed by violent impulses to kill herself "here and now").

A passage by Rainer Maria Rilke comes to mind:

> I am sure that "initiations" taught nothing but a "key" to reading the word "death" *without* a negative prefix. Like the moon, life has a face that we cannot see and that is *not* its opposite, but its complement, as it provides it with perfection and completeness, making it into an intact and whole sphere symbolizing *being.*[83]

The thirteenth card of the Tarot, Death, illustrates the same type of initiation:

> This playing card shows the well-known allegory of the skeleton with the difference that here, contrary to custom, he wields his scythe toward the left. And the bones of the skeleton are not grey but pink. The ground is strewn with human remains, but these remains, like those in legend and folklore, have the appearance of human beings—heads, for instance, keep their living expression; hands emerging from the ground seem ready for action. Everything in this enigma-card tends to ambivalence, underlining the fact that if life is, in itself, closely bound up with death . . . , death is also the source of life—and not only of spiritual life but of the resurrection of matter as well.[84]

In the Morgan-Greer Tarot deck, similar elements are imaged. The skeleton in the foreground carries a scythe, oriented toward the bottom left corner. In front of it is a rose in full bloom, white to symbolize pure love. In the background, a river (the flow of life) leading toward the dying sun is colored bright red.

Another image comes to mind, that of the double axe of Crete: here again, life and consciousnes on the right occur symmetrically with death

---

[83] *Briefe* [Letters], no. 373, to Countess Sizzo, June 1, 1923 (my translation).

[84] Cirlot, *Dictionary of Symbols,* p. 74.

and the unconscious on the left. We may also remember how initiation rites are said to give the novice the experience of being simultaneously alive and dead. Only by accepting this initiation can the ego feel truly contained in the Self; further, by finding the propitious attitude, it may succeed in overcoming the despair of Gethsemane.

I have stressed more than once that the propitious attitude need not be heroic. Despite Gethsemane, the Christian myth as a whole does not symbolize adequately the kind of attitude I have in mind. I shall thus introduce in the next chapter a myth from a tribal society, one that seems to provide a better analogy for what I mean.

6
God's Wretched Servants

The Father's Ambiguity

The following myth reformulates several themes introduced in chapters three, four and five, and describes very well what I call the propitious attitude. Its heroes adopt a nonheroic, pragmatic approach that allows them to survive, but that also implies giving up understanding or controlling their wretched situation. An abridged version will suffice to show the elements I am interested in:

> Once upon a time God sent down to earth His son to look into everything and advise on the possibility of creating living beings. At his father's orders the son left the sky and came down to the globe of the earth. But it was insufferably hot and he could not live anywhere, and so he plunged into the depths of the earth to find a little coolness. He never appeared again.
>
> God waited for a long time for his son to return. Uneasy at not seeing him, He sent servants to look for him. They were men who came to earth and each of them went a different way to try to find the missing person. But all their searching was fruitless.
>
> God's servants were wretched, for the earth was almost uninhabitable, it was so hot, so arid and so bare. Seeing the uselessness of their efforts, men sent from time to time one of their number to inform God of the failure of their search and to ask for fresh instructions. Numbers of men were thus despatched back to the Creator, but unluckily not one returned to earth. They are the dead.
>
> To this day messengers are still sent to Heaven since the son has not yet been found and no reply from God has reached the earth, where the first men settled and multiplied. They do not know what to do—should they go on looking or should they give up? Alas, not one of the messengers has returned to give us information on this point. And yet we still keep sending them, and the unsuccessful search continues.
>
> For this reason it is said that the dead never return to earth. But to reward mankind for their persistence in looking for His son, God sent rain to cool the earth and to allow His servants to cultivate the plants they need for food.[85]

---

[85] From the Malagasy; see Rosemary Gordon, *Dying and Creating: A Search for Meaning,* p. 71.

Rosemary Gordon writes that this myth expresses the human need to look for God and the fear of never finding Him. But it also speaks of the creation and maintenance of a communication channel between humans and God. Obviously, this channel is not used in a symmetrical manner: the messengers (the dead) are sent to Heaven, but God remains silent—or, rather, communicates only indirectly, by sending rain to cool the earth. However, it is essential that this channel remain open, because even indirect communication is indispensable to the group's survival.

A few parallels may be drawn with the Christian myth. Both narratives have in common the image of God's son being sent down to earth, the "messengers" (prayer in Christianity), the idea that the dead will eventually go back to Heaven or to God, and even the rather ambivalent nature of a Father who has lost His son (in Madagascar) or who had to make him an intermediary (in Christianity). In both cases, it is as if God were not able to interact directly with humans. In the tribal myth, one wonders at the men's continuing inability to find the son, whereas Christian man is clearly responsible for the Father's message being (not) understood. And yet in Madagascar these motifs reflect a very different existential atmosphere, due probably to the tribal culture that produced the myth as well as to drastically harsh environmental conditions.

Let us look at the different stages of the Malagasy myth, the creation first. Because God sends His son down to earth, man is created. Or, rather, the son is given the task of investigating such a creation and, after he does not come back, God is compelled to send His servants, that is, to create man. Can the loss of the son be interpreted as a kind of mishap on God's part, as a result of which man must be created? This creation does not really compensate the Father's loss, for the son remains missing; but the very fact of man's existence on earth at least allows the hope that one day the situation may change, and that God may recover His son.

On the other hand, human existence results from an accident, it is created almost by coincidence, and not because man is legitimately part of the Creation. What a contrast with the Western perception of the human race occupying the summit of a pyramid in which all other creatures are of lesser value!

The son vanishes into the depths of the earth and, with this, the only person who may have been able to inform man of the nature of God or of His intentions disappears. Does that make him the "Son on earth" of Christianity? If it does, it is only in such a way that despair must prevail: the search for the missing son remains unsuccessful. And yet, the very fact that he exists, somewhere within the bowels of the earth, makes it possible—more than that, makes it imperative—that a relationship should develop between humanity and the Father. The son's disappearance thus first provokes the creation of people and later leads them to find a solution to God's sorrow.

This God is not particularly threatening; He is worried about His son, a very human feeling. And humanity is not so much guilty—not having provoked the son's disappearance by breaking a taboo or by committing a sin—as responsible, in charge of the search, this being the very reason for their creation. This image of God may strike us, at least at first, as rather un-godlike. Of course, the Father is availed of a certain power, but He is unable to use it in order to find His own son and has to rely on humans. In this sense, His behavior is rather unclear: he cannot any longer function without people, but why did he put Himself in this situation?

Humanity's anxiety at not being able to find God's son is thus paralleled by the Father's inability to bring him back. This symmetry—both are powerless, if not really condemned to impotence—together with the despair they share moves God and humans to conclude a pact; they become interdependent. We find here, as in the Christian Incarnation, the notion of a Godhead who cannot be (divine) without being granted a reflection in the human soul, that is, the idea of God's relativity.

What do humans do in this terrible situation, faced with a God in sorrow whose reaction may, after all, be rather unpredictable? In fact, they do what they can, and no more, unsure of the results. Human beings send messengers to Heaven, not in order to bring good news, but simply to keep God informed. This is far from the idea that man must do good to please or placate God, and even farther from the image of a symbiotic, paradisiac fusion between the human race and God, provided that man does what God wants.

In psychological terms, the Malagasy myth pictures a very tenuous relationship between the ego and the Self: the ego's instinctive need to be part of a transcendent entity seems to remain, in part, unsatisfied. The Self symbolized by this Father who has lost His son is, as such, less than perfect. It has neither power nor absolute knowledge and cannot solve its own problem; further, God cannot cope alone with the suffering and worry provoked by the loss.

And yet, despite the Self's imperfect nature and despite the ego's frustrated longing for the safety of a blissful relationship with a loving god, humanity survives. More, new life is created. But the situation remains precarious: what would happen if God suddenly got angry or lost patience? And how can humans live on this arid, barren earth?

I wonder whether the first dead, beyond their function of reporting on the failure of the search, were not also sent to get advice from God, the Creator, on how to live in His creation. However, there was soon no need for anxiety about this aspect of the problem, since the persistence of these first searchers in looking for the Son was rewarded by rain, so it became possible to grow food.

Indeed, this is the truly paradoxical element in the myth: an obscure move, an uncertain attempt at modifying a desperate situation, does not bring a solution, but it does allow individuals to adapt to the situation, despite the son not having been found. This move, of course, is accompanied by another: not only is the search for the son continued, but, in the meantime, messengers are sent at regular intervals. Both aspects are interdependent, for there would be no need for a progress report if the search did not go on. And, inversely, what would become of the relationship between God and humans if the son were found?

On the other hand, the despatching of messengers is not just a gratuitous gesture, since it implies that these will be lost to the group. But here, Thanatos as one pole of the Self is neither instinct nor drive; it is a last resource, a means of keeping in touch with God. The need for death is partially clear: humanity knows why the messengers must go, but not why they do not come back. Of course, one may see this passage, or even the whole myth, as an attempt at explaining death. That would be one possible interpretation; but there is also the moral element: humanity must feel at least partially responsible for death, since the search for the son has remained unsuccessful. And yet, death is not seen as a punishment for breaking a taboo, nor as the willful revenge of a moody God. It has a function, preventing the situation from getting worse. What is more, God shares the responsibility: after all, why did He have to go and lose His son, and why can't He find him Himself?

More importantly still, the sacrifice effected each time a messenger is sent to Heaven seems to bring results: the earth becomes less barren, the rain allows God's servants to cultivate the plants they need for food. For this reason, there really is no alternative. Humans must see that even though it may not make the situation less precarious, the attempt to cope cannot be entirely wrong. The earth carries the fruits of life, making it possible to survive under these conditions. Put in more abstract terms, the acceptance of death allows humanity to remain in contact with a transcendent deity and thus to live.

Let us move to a more psychological level and look for parallels rather than contrasts between the Christian and the Malagasy myths, in particular with regard to the relationship between the ego and the Self. But first, another fundamental difference deserves mention. The idea of a Savior, such as was incarnated in Christ after the Crucifixion, is missing from the tribal myth. Or, rather, this Son of God around whom the whole story revolves is strangely absent, having disappeared into the depths of the earth, into the unconscious. He was delegated by God to investigate the possibility of creating living beings, apparently because the Father was unable to do this Himself (though the story does not tell us why). As in Christianity, it is thus the Son who serves as the primary link in the chain that connects the Godhead and humanity—and this may be no small part of the Son's redeeming function. But in Madagascar, after this initial stage, it is enough that he exists—and that he remains inaccessible. We are very far from the idea of Christ as a model to imitate or as a Savior.

Psychologically speaking, the Malagasy Son of God represents a dynamic element in the Self that is more personal and less archetypal than the Father residing in a remote Heaven. He is the *imago dei* buried in the depths of the unconscious that the Self, as the archetype of a transcendent dimension, forces us to search for, so that a relationship between the ego and the Godhead might develop. In the abridged version of the myth I presented, neither the Father nor the Son is described. In particular, very little is said about God's nature or intentions. But both have anthropoid characteristics, with the behavior one would expect from a human father and son. God, on the other hand, is strangely devoid of the qualities that in most tribal religions characterize the deities: strength, supernatural powers, the ability to control the cosmos. He corresponds to an unusual type of projection of the *imago dei,* one that leaves us with great freedom and responsibility. We ourselves must discover how to relate to this particular Godhead.

Such a relationship parallels the Self's dependence on the ego to realize itself. The Self may suggest what the ego should do, and can, up to a certain point, impose its will on the ego by provoking neurosis and other symptoms when the ego's attitude does not correspond to its intentions.

But finally it is always the ego, the conscious standpoint, that must choose to accept the Self's guidance or rebel. It is true, however, that the ego's choice may not, in the last resort, be as free as it may like to believe.

Describing the options open to the ego when confronted with the Self's will, Jung used a metaphor:

> It is the task of the conscious mind to understand these hints [from the unconscious]. If this does not happen, the process of individuation will nevertheless continue. The only difference is that we become its victims and are dragged along by fate toward that inescapable goal which we might have reached walking upright, if only we had taken the trouble and been patient enough to understand in time the meaning of the numina that cross our path.[86]

In the Malagasy myth, people have few alternatives, and the situation requires urgent action. At first, the action taken is not very conscious. A first "blind" attempt at facing the anxiety involved in God's loss seems to bear fruit and humanity starts hoping that the Father is satisfied. But is this not also a basic psychological experience? When in a quandary, we may of course take concrete action. We may also work on dreams, or do some creative work without knowing in advance whether it is the right thing to do or where it will take us. Or we may decide to do nothing and wait, relinquishing the desire for an immediate solution. Then something may happen, energies will be set in motion, better feelings about the situation may arise. Is it really necessary that we should know exactly what happened, or how it worked? Do we need more than the experience of the earth being fertilized by rain?

A few more aspects of the ego-Self relationship symbolized in the myth may be transferred to our everyday reality. First, in spite of the familiarity that progressively enters the relation between humans and the Father, some uncertainty remains: we can never be quite sure we have done the right thing, and the situation remains precarious. Second, the Father's obscure behavior corresponds to the unclear nature of the numinous as a transcendent power that includes a *tremendum* and a *fascinans,* inspiring both fear and enchantment.[87] Were this dimension absent, individuals might decide to stop "working," forgetting to maintain the communication channel with God or abandoning the search for His son. With this dimen-

---

[86] "Answer to Job," *Psychology and Religion,* CW 11, par. 746.

[87] See Rudolf Otto, *The Idea of the Holy: An Inquiry into the Non-Rational Factor in the Idea of the Divine and Its Relation to the Rational.*

sion present, even though our Malagasy tribe can reasonably assume that they have discovered the right attitude, the persistent threat of unforesee-able events keeps them trying.

This indeterminacy is also found in the confrontation with the Self at the level of individual psychology. As an archetype, the Self is numinous and contains both terrifying and fascinating energies. Thus, the only possible attitude toward its power is one in which the ego may never be too sure that it has "arrived," right and secure. This requires humility on the part of the ego toward the transcendent power inherent in the Self. It may also be a requirement for on-going vitality, for meeting life's constant changes.

Furthermore, the Malagasy tribe must go on "paying the price" of a security that is temporary. The dead have to be sacrificed so that the situation remains bearable. They must also accept their ignorance of why this is so and the need to keep performing an apparently absurd gesture, knowing that their messengers will not return.

One may object that they trade death for life, since fertility comes to the earth as if in exchange for the dead. To my mind, however, the fertility is not a direct reward for sending the dead, but a manifestation of God's satisfaction with their attitude, or even an expression of His need to allow humanity to remain on earth in order to carry on the search for the Son. Of course tribal groups knew their members would die—whether or not they believed that the dead may return. The myth may image this knowledge. But, psychologically speaking, this image expresses another dimension: the ego must sacrifice part of itself, despite the apparent absurdity of this gesture, because this sacrifice allows it to remain in contact with the Self and to insure that the relation is positive enough for life to continue. Symbolically, the ego must acknowledge death in order to live fully.

This may be one point where the negative pole of the Self is expressed in the myth. In that sense, we may see it as the moving force behind the sacrifice. However, the dark Self also manifests in the original heat and aridity of the earth. Unbearable temperatures and the absence of fertility are part of the original cosmos, requiring even the Father Himself to wonder whether He may extend His Creation to such an inadequate environment. It is as if God were confronted with the problem of the shadow, facing potential destruction or at least impotence.

This view is confirmed by the fact that in the myth God is almost as helpless as humans. Later, the Father sends rain and the tribe survives. But one part of the cosmos, of the original Self, can revert to a desert inimical to life. Thus the myth clearly expresses the destructive aspect of nature, on which tribes remain totally dependent. God, or the Self, is not only not loving toward man, He is also faced with His own dark side.

Further, the Father keeps the messengers as hostages, or just remains silent in a precarious situation that remains precarious; both are actions that are inimical to humans, leaving them in a quandary similar to Christ's in Gethsemane: God demands death as much as He gives life. However, the myth stresses not so much the revengeful, threatening nature of God as His inability to act differently. The Father is worried, having lost His son, and the dead are His own servants. How could one expect Him to behave differently?

As opposed to the Christian myth, this story stresses the uncertain consequences for humankind of unavoidable limitations in the Godhead. God's ambivalence is perfectly natural; in the face of His own situation, what alternatives does He have? Here, as in Gethsemane, individuals can only accept this ambivalence, despite their suffering and doubts. Tribal groups did not for one moment expect the gods to love them without restriction; they accepted the double nature of the gods, destructive as well as nourishing, without hesitation.

This simple acceptance, though it may be motivated more by pragmatism than by conscious choice, prevents the dark pole from gaining the upper hand. The earth will be fertile, and relations with the Father will be such that guarded hope may continue. In this sense, the Malagasy God is a complete deity, neither very loving nor too evil, who has not been split; indeed, humans may feel more contained by Him than by the Father of Gethsemane, a father whose nature had been turned more black and white by Jesus' belief in the triumph of good over evil. Madagascar tribal members are not preoccupied by moral considerations, nor do they try fundamentally to transform the situation. They surrender control, moved by an obscure instinct, for reasons that probably remain unclear to them and involve submission to cycles of death, doubt and wretchedness. But they have found something that corresponds rather well to the right attitude of the ego toward the Self, the proper ego-Self relation as it has been described by Jung.[88] Furthermore, their surrender insures that they continue to find their just place within the cosmos.

Before relating the propitious attitude to some aspects of the Malagasy

---

[88] See above, chap. five.

myth, I wish to explain why I am using it as a model. The split in the God-image created by the Judeo-Christian tradition is a reality that greatly influences the Western collective psyche, and this situation will not change simply by substituting another myth. Yet, in my everyday practice, I have to find a pragmatic approach that may help my analysands face the dark side of God. In using the Malagasy myth, I am using one possible amplification of the psychic situation in which these analysands find themselves after they have given up defending against, splitting and repressing the dark pole of the Self. It is a threatening, ambiguous situation that cannot adequately be dealt with by using contemporary Western models.

In my experience, once the analytic process has helped these analysands relate to the deeper layers of the unconscious, amplifications that allow them (temporarily) to gain some distance from their conscious or unconscious Judeo-Christian inheritance make it easier for them to accept the dark and to discover a propitious attitude. And, up to a certain point, the world really is what we make it; that is, our inner attitude, the way we write our own myth, greatly influences the way we are in the world. In that sense, I find the god and the attitude described by the Malagasy myth to be very helpful with regard to psychic reality.

The Propitious Attitude

I would like to return, on a more concrete level, to specific dimensions of the propitious attitude. First I will relate them to the Malagasy myth, and then examine their place within individual psychology and everyday analytic practice.

The first dimension is that of persistence, of the unflinching will to seek out and confront the unknown. In the Madagascar myth, humans at first seem to have no choice: the Father has made them, His servants, responsible for finding the Son. Later the tribe has an alternative, since they may give up after their efforts produce no direct results. But they go on searching, and thanks to this stubbornness the earth becomes fruitful.

This quality was prominent in Perceval's quest as well. The very fact of his being "on his way," his willingness to act even if it did not lead immediately to finding the treasure, is enough to free blocked energies and recover some vitality for the psyche. When finally Perceval the Fool asks the innocent question, "Whom does the Grail serve?" the land regains its fertility. In the Malagasy myth, there is no question to be asked, but the very absence of a question is significant: the tribe has to accept the incomprehensible, and not even try to understand it. In both narratives, the search is more important than its aim.

Does this not apply psychologically as well? Whether we choose to understand as much as possible, or renounce rational explanation and trust the "fool," in either case and as soon as some (ritual) work is invested, psychic energy is released. What was blocked, or seemed immutable, cannot stay that way, since new elements have entered the picture. In Andreij Tarkowskij's film *Offret* (Sacrifice, 1986) a novice is told by an old monk to water an apparently dead tree on a hill. The novice obeys, although it takes him almost the whole day, every day, to carry one bucket of water to the top of the hill on which the dead tree stands. After three years, the tree starts growing leaves . . .

One may object that above reflections are banal or obvious. But it is not so easy for either analysand or analyst to accept that in certain phases of the process their task is—must be—just like that carried out by this novice *and* that this apparently nonsensical act is psychologically essential.

Analysts are sometimes tempted to eliminate insecurity by putting each case within the framework of a ready-made theoretical model. If we are not careful, we may start seeing in a client only the characteristics described by rational psychological categories and stop searching. Further, we sometimes go as far as to use Jung's very flexible paradigms of the psyche and its irrationality as a fixed, mechanistic system, within which a specific symbol automatically calls for a specific interpretation. We tend to see this system as endowed with the capacity to evolve in a linear, almost predictable manner, forgetting that this is our own bias.

Perceval's quest, as well as the Malagasy search or the characteristics of the marginal period of initiation rituals, clearly show that these tendencies need to be balanced by an attitude that sees the path as far less clearly defined, or less direct. Analysis must be a quest, as much for the analyst as for the analysand. An affinity for Eros and the fool, together with an acceptance of penumbra and *circumambulatio,* with all their paradoxes and contradictions, support the propitious attitude. (One might remember the image of the boat sailing in concentric circles *around* the island in Miguel's dream.)

This attitude, by including the imaginary world, leaves space for feeling, emotion and nonrational thinking. It is with the heart that one imagines. An attitude in which the process is seen as a quest through unknown territory rather than through already-mapped terrain allows both analysand

and analyst to accept developments that, from a collective perspective and within the frame of rigid models, would be considered a mistake. Again, finding B while looking for A . . .

The second dimension of the propitious attitude, that of patient surrender to the confrontation with frightening elements, is clearly expressed in the Malagasy myth. It is akin to the "reversal of reality" accepted during the marginal period of initiation. The tribe has to accept the loss, the sacrifice even, of the dead, in order to survive. The ego must partly renounce its own cosmos, so that it can stay in contact with the Self. It will also need to accept that the basic situation will remain the same. The "work" involved in the search for the son will always have do be done anew, the dead will always have to be sacrificed.

It seems to me, with regard to analytic practice, that this dimension corresponds to an attitude focused more on accommodating to the present than on an optimistic view of the future. For both parties in the analytic relationship, it gives up any promise of better times in which pain and doubt will vanish. This attitude results from choosing to live *in spite of* suffering and uncertainty. Patrick, for instance, is still experiencing a constant struggle; but he has stopped being a victim. Thus, though this perspective may seem pessimistic, it is fundamentally realistic. We have seen that it must also include a respect for the transpersonal forces at work and the avoidance of fascination or identification with the negative. Under these conditions, it may serve as a basis for the acceptance of a personal destiny, transforming the analysand's existential situation by making it more than merely bearable, if not necessarily positive in collective terms.

Of course the analyst may unconsciously prefer to promise a cure, or at least give grounds for hope, trying to lead the client away from pain and doubt. It is difficult to tell someone that despair is justified and that perhaps meaning is to be found *in* the suffering, not beyond it. But my experience convinces me that if we fall prey to the temptation of promising a cure, we simply rob the psyche of a way of confronting darkness. In this sense, we may need to surrender *with* our analysands, and suffer with them from not being able to offer any solutions; we ourselves need to practice the patient acceptance that, we hope, will allow passage to another stage.

I will digress here briefly, to examine the relationship between hope and despair in analysis and their influence on the work.

Obviously, as I stressed earlier, hope is a potent antidote to suffering. Also, it is because one hopes for a positive change that one starts analysis in the first place, and hope will certainly contribute to the process. One may need to be careful not to attribute less importance to this dimension than in fact it has, but it should also be placed within a realistic perspective. The analysand's hope may be too much of an illusion, when for example one believes that a few sessions will eliminate the pain. Then the problem is to ground the hope on a stronger foundation. Sometimes hope expresses itself through an extreme need for concretization ("If I change this or that aspect of my life—my job, my partner—then I'll be fine"). In this case, interiorization should be encouraged. In each case, neither analysand nor analyst need give up hope. But their hope must be channeled in such a way that it will serve as a motor to the analytic process.

According to Jung psychic events always have an aim, a *telos*. By encouraging the analysand to recognize and to respect the psyche's intentions, we help develop the feeling of being supported by a transcendent entity. Of course, and in particular with the cases we are interested in here, the psyche's aim or the path it chooses may not look as positive as the client may hope. But an awareness of underlying forces and an acceptance of the irrational reveal the soul's dynamic nature. This dynamism, which James Hillman calls a "sense of purpose" and which he relates to a movement toward the future,[89] is what carries the analysand's hope. In this sense, one may hope, not for specific aims such as progress, individuation or the elimination of symptoms, but for a movement within the psyche that makes the analytic process vital. In other words, the feeling of living in harmony with one's personal fate is, in itself, therapeutic. Together with the sense of purpose mentioned above, hope then counteracts resignation.

The despair of the analyst constitutes another dynamic component in the transference-countertransference relationship.[90] Within this dynamic, despair can be part of a fruitful analysis if, through emotions, the analyst joins the client on an archetypal level. However, the despair and its function may be insufficiently understood if they are seen only as a sharing of the analysand's feeling of being in a hopeless situation. In this sense, the analyst would help the client carry the burden by despairing *with*. Further, by really seeing and accepting the dark sides of the analysand's life, the analyst can show they have value.

---

[89] *Archetypal Psychology,* p. 43.
[90] See Ph. Rupp, "Die Verzweiflung des Analytikers: Ein Versuch ihrer Darstellung und Erklärung" [The Analyst's Despair: A Descriptive and Explanatory Essay].

These mechanisms may well play a role in any analysis. But it seems to me that the despair of the analyst also has a larger impact. First, it gives dynamism to the blocked energies that force the analysand to submit passively to a negative fate or to identify with the darkest traits in his or her personality. From the moment the analyst starts genuinely to despair, the *status quo* is broken, allowing the hope that something may happen through the transference.

The analyst's admission of despair may also force the client to take a position vis-à-vis the threatening forces. On the basis of experience, the analyst will likely be able to face the lack of hope in a more focused, active manner than the analysand can. The client's despair may thus find new forms or new means of expression. At the same time, the analysand may observe and be influenced by the manner in which the analyst works on his or her own despair, if only unconsciously. This will provide the analysand with a model for possible new paths of action.

Furthermore, in accord with psychic compensation and *enantiodromia,* the despair shared by analyst and analysand may constellate other unconscious forces. It will corner the psyche, so to speak, into offering new solutions. Here, a dynamic relationship at the level of the unconscious may guide the analytic process along new lines. The analyst stops being the almighty healer and must trust suprapersonal elements to intervene; in turn, the analysand has to give up a one-sidedly hopeless perspective.

And finally, what was said above about hope and the psyche's purposiveness also applies to despair. By encouraging the analysand to take an interest in his or her own soul and in the purpose of life, the analyst may help the other discover the meaning even in very negative symptoms, and thus also to accept moments of despair.

Concerning the matter of surrender as a helpful reversal of attitude, an aspect of the tribal rites of passage comes back to mind: the reversal of everyday life, in which diametrically opposed dimensions coexist.

It may well be that the refusal to promise better days to the analysand truly reverses the collective attitude dominant in the West, from which many clients have already suffered. The positive norms of health and happiness are terribly cruel to those who do not meet them. Further, they promote guilt ("Since everyone else is healthy and happy, I must have committed some terrible sin").

Indeed, the psychotic's or schizophrenic's suffering results less from the frightening impact of visions than from the feeling of being excluded from a society unable to share them. Their pain is that of being deprived of interaction, of being pushed to the edges of the group. As for neurotic individuals, they often suffer from the feeling that others do not accept them. With regard to analysis, the alienation felt by the psychotic or the neurotic may be seen as a state like that of the novice, in which naive instinctive action must be taken in order to avoid total despair. And this may well involve, for the analyst, an acceptance of a momentarily reversed reality.

We have seen that the novice enduring the marginal phase of initiation, and the innocent of the folktale, must enter into contact with the divine child, with the instinctively complete symbol of the Self. This aspect is not expressed clearly in the Malagasy myth but it is implied. The tribe confronting its difficult existential situation cannot rely on conscious, rational decisions to survive. It needs to react instinctively and take apparently absurd action, like Lucky Hans, in order to avoid despair. This need even presses the tribe to do something that looks really foolish, since it keeps on knowingly sending messengers in vain. By the same token, Lucky Hans's bargains seemed foolish, short-changing him rather than helping him return home a rich man.

The child who guides this type of reaction is connected with the unconscious, with nature and with instinct. In spite of our professional work with the unconscious we often remain too close to collective norms, materialistic values, and ideas of efficiency and progress, to see what may genuinely be inspired by this child in an analysand's behavior. We are tempted to apply a model, to work within norms that are concerned, on the one hand, with what is allowed—behaviors that are considered healthy—and on the other, with what should be—the manner in which, within a Jungian model, conscious and unconscious should relate. Have we not forgotten the simplicity that would allow us to accept that for certain analysands, things simply are as they are *and* that it may be just as well that they are? Have we not forgotten that the psyche has its own intentions?

Specifically I question designating as "symptoms" or "resistances" those behaviors that do not fit our developmental or analytic model. We are sometimes too impatient to "make conscious," to "integrate," or to "help mature and differentiate." Of course, I am not advocating total freedom; the analysand lives within a society and the limits of what may be accepted lie at the point where behavior may be prejudicial to other people. But at the imaginary level so essential to our work, everything must be allowed and everything must be accepted. And, at a more everyday level, the moment when an absolute open-mindedness may need to be replaced by a more active, intervening attitude should also be chosen according to the degree to which the analysand suffers from the concrete situation. However, if we accept that the suffering does not need to be only negative, this moment may well come later than we sometimes think.

Further, if the analyst is not personally in contact with the archetype of the divine child, he or she cannot help constellate this archetype in the client. If we work within the frameworks formulated by the fathers, within an evaluating and selective perspective, we shall not be able to help our analysands reconnect with a containing, nourishing mother. We have seen that, in the divine child, both poles, light and darkness, conscious and unconscious, life and death, are very close to each other. The child "knows" because it contains both poles. Only this archetype can help heal the split resulting from a dichotomization or partial identification with one or the other pole of the Self.

This does not mean that the analyst's role is only to mother the child, or to concentrate on the more childlike side of the analysand. The temptation to do so may well come from the unconscious preferences I have described above. There may be moments when a good deal of mothering will not go amiss, and I am not saying that the analyst should be cruel. But mothering can bring the work further only if, at the same time, a nonregressive childlike attitude is being constellated. It will lead further only on condition that the analyst does not use the relationship "mother-mirroring-narcissistic-child" as a model in which too little space is left for the psyche's spontaneous expression. The use of any theoretical model may bring a blockage as soon as it ceases being extremely flexible. Thus, the child *must* be there, but in its archetypal dimensions. And the work must be focused on the future rather than on the causalities of the past.

The return to the "land of childhood" is healing only when it goes beyond trying to repair the "faults" that have been traced back. If anything, a regression to childhood must allow analysands to reexperience the emotions involved and, by integrating them into current life, help them bear fruit in the future. But they cannot be eliminated by a new developmental process effected through the analysis. I must admit that I have difficulties seeing these emotions as simply providing causal explanations. I sometimes wonder whether the fashionable models of therapy that focus on mirroring are not influenced by the idealization of childhood that seems characteristic of our times. At this level, the child has become an imago, remote—and sometimes cut off—from its archetypal roots. It is to these roots that the analytic relationship needs to relate, not to the contemporary actualization of the child archetype.

As for the lack of a stable ego in some analysands, I would say that it is precisely those with a defective ego-Self axis who, even more than others, need to reconnect with the less differentiated, more primitive contents of the psyche that are much closer to the Self. If the analyst is able to use enough sensitivity and empathy, the ego need not react by blocking, defending or decompensating. A large part of the process may take place at an archetypal, symbolic level, remaining impersonal for as long as necessary. The process may also develop in the background and remain inexplicit, "unanalyzed," while the transference-countertransference directs it along the right path. Not everything has to be be put into words, especially for a fragile ego.

The final dimension of the propitious attitude, that of the unavoidable confrontation with a cosmos and a Self having both light *and* dark (destructive, but also unfathomable) aspects, is given by the very nature of the Self. As I have stressed, this confrontation is indispensable to any passage toward another stage. Also, without it there cannot be any vitality. We have seen, in relation to Mary's case, that the avoidance of this aspect can easily lead to partial suicide. What is more, although I have been implicitly criticizing a perception of the Self that makes it a "loving inner guide," the Self can still show one how to cope with the dark: it knows more about this dimension than the ego that refuses to relate to it.

Let me return to the Malagasy myth. There the negative pole is rather implicit; the earth is barren and death must be accepted, but God is not said to be malevolent as such. We have seen that the attitude encoded by the myth lets the tribe live with the dark pole and thereby attenuates its threat. In other words, humanity tries to live this wretched situation, no more and no less; but with success, objective reality changes and the earth provides food. The initial task, that of searching for the son in order to avoid provoking the wrath of an unpredictable Father, modifies the cosmos; an unforeseen evolution takes place. A hesitant, almost fearful gesture provokes unexpected and partly beneficial results.

This stands in striking contrast with the hero's cutting off the dragon's head or with the analytic attitude that sees the relation to the Self as resting on a clear, conscious perception of the mechanisms involved, and relies on a will to progress toward more differentiation and more consciousness.

I firmly believe that a genuine analytic approach must accept that answers might come from the Devil, or that the Grail can be found without carrying a sword, perhaps even without knowing who the Devil is or what the Grail promises. The analyst must be able to accompany the client's search without really understanding why certain galaxies are the way they are or why black holes exist, by simply observing the effect of the measures taken, or the reaction coming from the chaos of the Self, and by participating in this action-reaction through the emotions constellated in the transference-countertransference relationship. Analytic work must accommodate itself to mystery and to shadows; it must accept them, especially when it becomes clear that, visibly, the earth is becoming less of a desert and the analysand's energies begin to flow again.

The tension between Eros and Thanatos, between the vital and the morbid aspects of being, will always remain. But it can be accepted, resolutely and with open eyes. Both analyst and analysand may thus choose to proceed with the client's destiny rather than try to modify it. They may also deliberately surrender to Eros in its entirety, including its dark, irrational and threatening aspects.

Of course, for the analyst, renouncing the security of progress-centered aims may bring a feeling that his or her work is inefficient. The analyst stops being all-knowing, the one who can repair the soul and show the way out of the shadows. The healer archetype is comforting, but it may also seduce one with its power. It may not be easy for the analyst to accept practicing a trade from which notions such as success, progress and achievement have been eliminated.

Obviously, the acceptance and sharing of the analysand's pain, the confrontation with sinister, dispiriting or even desperate moments in the analytic relationship, may also involve another risk. When the analysand's psyche chooses a path close to that followed by the Iglulik novice, it can be relatively easy for both partners to share the weeks or the months of patient meditation. But what happens in cases of progressive disintegration, the rotting away of Inanna's flesh on the stake? How loud will the analysand's screams of pain be? And where will the rage provoked by a feeling of absolute helplessness be directed, if not toward the analyst? In this sense, the right surrender may involve risks for the analyst, who stops being the loving mother and takes on a negative role.

Whatever form the process of confrontation with the dark Self may take, the analyst's aim is, of course, still to support the contact between the analysand's consciousness and the deeper layers of the psyche, so that an inadequately formed ego-Self axis may redevelop on a stronger basis. It is also to help the analysand relate to his or her own soul, to the psyche that shapes one's fate. As we have seen in chapter three, one way to intervene along this axis is through imaginary representations.

Narratives, symbols and the marginal period of rituals are powerful means of communication between the ego and the Self, and between the individual and the collective. They carry healing potential. In a developmental approach, where the analyst brings the analysand back through the various stages, primacy is given to the ego: the ego is seen as requiring "treatment." In the perspective I am discussing, priority is assigned to the Self and its archetypal level, that is, to the ritual work through which this level can be contacted. The analytic exchange takes place in the language of the *mundus imaginalis*. The (silent) dialogue circles around the Self and aims at allowing the analysand to feel safe within a sufficiently complete archetype, so that it can serve as a strong basis for a new separation of the ego along the ego-Self axis. There is a return to the Self, so that the ego gets a chance to experience it in a more complete manner and eventually to feel contained by it in a way better suited to existential experience.

I have here reached the limit of what I am able to verbalize, and there may be intrinsic reasons for this. First, much of what happens in the analytic vessel really is of an entirely nonverbal nature; it is also fluid and not easily trapped in schemas. A model can serve only as a global frame. It can only schematize—and influence—the atmosphere in which the exchange takes place, but it will never give proper account of the (al)chemistry of the sessions. Second, and this plays a far greater role, the questions I have touched on are part of a fundamental interrogation with a much larger scope. Attempting to define the propitious attitude toward the Self implies a deeper reflection on the place of humanity in the cosmos *and* the place of analysis within that context.

Both issues, the ultimate function of analysis and the fluidity of its contents, are best reflected on by the analyst in privacy. The very verbalization of these topics structures the reflection more than the concrete work requires; it may even hamper the spontaneous emotional reactions that are so essential to the transference-countertransference relationship. A genuinely analytic attitude includes the ability to stand the tension between a need to understand and structure and the knowledge that the nature of the psyche will always interfere with this need. It must also realize that each case is different and follows its own dynamics. As Jung wrote (referring to the problem of the shadow, but I believe his observation is also relevant to the role of the analyst):

> There is nothing that I can do *except wait, with a certain trust in God,* until, out of a conflict borne with patience and fortitude, there emerges the solution destined—although I cannot foresee it—for that particular person. Not that I am passive or inactive meanwhile.[91]

My attempt to define the propitious attitude is only aimed at finding a means to bear the conflict "with patience and fortitude." I am also trying to compensate for the conscious standpoint's natural tendency to be active, to broaden itself, and to refuse to surrender rational control of the situation, for this tendency compromises the propitious attitude.

Nevertheless, defining a propitious attitude may, in itself, involve the risk that, as the elements inherent to the confrontation with the dark are being labeled and more consciously perceived, the ego, whether analyst's or analysand's, will fall prey to the illusion of being able to understand and, again, to control. Furthermore, it would be wrong to believe that recognizing the dark will inevitably serve consciousness; we have seen that completely integrating the shadow is an impossible endeavor. Facing the dark Self in the terms I have described should be understood as a means for the ego to cope with the situation in which it finds itself, not as a way of eliminating darkness; this is an important distinction.

Also, as we saw with respect to actually living with the despair of Gethsemane, it would be wrong, although maybe tempting, to believe that a Resurrection following the Crucifixion has been foreseen by a God who is, after all, loving. It would be wrong, too, to hope that an acceptance of the dark Self can be used to bring more light, that its contents may be controlled by Logos.

What I have in mind, deriving from my experience with analysands, is rather that this acceptance brings a new form of consciousness that is, in fact, akin to a nonconsciousness. It brings a nonrational *awareness* of psychic reality which corresponds more adequately to the nature of the soul than is generally understood by the term "consciousness." It applies the form of thinking characteristic of the *natural mind,* the spirit of nature that tells the truth without relying on book knowledge.

The myth of the Malagasy may be used here again. Once it is accepted

---

[91] *Psychology and Alchemy,* CW 12, par. 37 (emphasis added).

that God or the cosmos is not only good, *and* that nothing one does will modify this fundamental fact, one can find the means of living in such a cosmos and a way of relating to its deities. This does not bring an understanding of what God wants or of what the cosmos is, nor even the certainty that God's intentions are loving; but it does allow survival and gives one a place in the world.

At a psychological level, accepting and facing the dark Self does not bring happiness, and whenever it brings the hope that light may triumph over darkness, this hope is either an illusion or the result of an inflation. Nevertheless, in my experience it does bring peace.

A transformation takes place in which the analysand may acquire an intuitive knowledge of the world—I am tempted to write "an almost cosmic consciousness"—that allows one to *feel* (to know, in the sense of *gnosis,* without understanding) that he or she has a place, a *just place* in the cosmos. One no longer feels like a victim of nefarious powers and discovers a place along a transcendent, sacred continuum that reaches far beyond personal, linear time. The longing for a Godhead able to contain and to accompany everyday existence, for a God who may comfort and relieve existential fears, is fulfilled through the experience of this participation. According to Hillman,[92] one is then in contact with the *anima mundi*, with the cosmic psyche, and this contact relieves existential tension.

These remarks may sound mystical, but it is difficult to use a different tone when talking of problems that reach into the very roots of life. At a more concrete, everyday level, we may simply say that the propitious attitude toward the Self may be seen as a means of helping an individual reach this form of consciousness, away from the norms defining progress, reason or normality. Thus one takes responsibility for one's own vitality and experiences it in a subjective manner. I would say that psychic health is just that: the ability to go with one's personal fate, to fully accept it, even if it seems rather negative and brings suffering.

The image of the novice's stones comes back, with all its simplicity and depth. The slow, patient work of rubbing, through which the stones imperceptibly wear down until their monotonous song allows the novice to contact the "bones" of life—the skeleton carrying both life and eternity—and lets him reconnect with a fundamental, primitive source. According to Jung, this "reversion to the primitive,"

---

[92] *Archetypal Psychology,* p. 43.

or, as in India, the uninterrupted connection with it, keeps man in touch with Mother Earth, the prime source of all power. Seen from the heights of a differentiated point of view, whether rational or ethical, these instinctive forces are "impure." But life itself flows from springs both clear and muddy. Hence all excessive "purity" lacks vitality. A constant striving for clarity and differentiation means a proportional loss of vital intensity, precisely because the muddy elements are excluded. Every renewal of life needs the muddy as well as the clear.[93]

---

[93] *Psychological Types*, CW 6, par. 415.

Bibliography

Aarne, A., and Thompson, S. *The Types of the Folktale.* Helsinki: Folklore Fellow Communications, No. 184, 1961.

Ammann, R. "Healing and Transformation in Sandplay." Trans. W.-D. Rainer. Foreword by Donald Sandner. La Salle, IL: Open Court, 1991.

Barth, K., *Die kirchliche Dogmatik IV—Die Lehre der Versöhnung.* Teil 1. Zürich: Evangelischer Verlag, 1953. *[Church Dogmatics, vol. 4—Doctrine of Reconciliation.* Part 1. Trans. and ed. G.W. Bromiley and T.F. Torrance. London: T. and T. Clark, 1962.]

Bash, K.W. "Hemisphärenharmonie." [Hemispheric Harmony]. *Analytic. Psychol.,* 16: 276-301 (1985).

Bleuler, Eugen. "Das autistische Denken" [Autistic Thinking]. *Jahrbuch psychoanalyt. psychopath,* Forschung 4: 1-39 (1912).

_____. *Lehrbuch der Psychiatrie.* Ed. Manfred Bleuler. Berlin: Springer, 1983. *[Textbook of Psychiatry.* Reprint of 1924 ed. Salem, NH: Ayer, 1976.]

Cirlot, J.E. *A Dictionary of Symbols.* London: Routledge and Kegan Paul, 1962.

Dallett, Janet O. *Saturday's Child: Encounters with the Dark Gods.* Toronto: Inner City Books, 199

de Beauvoir, Simone. *All Men Are Mortal.* New York: Norton, 1992.

de Troyes, Chrétien. *The Story of the Grail.* Trans. R.W. Linker. Chapel Hill: University of North Carolina Press, 1952.

Durand, G. *Les structures anthropologiques de l'imaginaire: introduction à l'archétypologie générale* [The Anthropological Structures of Imagination: Introduction to General Archetypology]. Paris: Bordas, 1979.

Edinger, Edward F. *Transformation of the God-Image: An Elucidation of Jung's* Answer to Job. Toronto: Inner City Books, 1992.

Eliade, Mircea. *The Myth of the Eternal Return* (Bollingen Series LXVI). Trans. W.R. Trask. Princeton: Princeton University Press, 1954.

_____. *The Sacred and the Profane.* Trans. W.R. Trask. New York: Harper Brace Jovanovich, 1959.

_____. *Shamanism: Archaic Techniques of Ecstasy* (Bollingen Series LXXVI). Trans. W.R. Trask. Princeton: Princeton University Press, 1964.

Firth, R. *We, the Tikopia.* London: Allen and Unwin, 1936.

Fordham, M. "Notes on the Transference." In *Techniques in Jungian Analysis.* The Library of Analytical Psychology, vol. 2. London: William Heinemann Medical Books, 1974.

Francot, Enrico. "Das eisige Selbst—ein Versuch" [The Icy Self—an Essay]. In *Gorgo,* no. 23 (1992).

Gordon, Rosemary. *Dying and Creating: A Search for Meaning.* The Library of Analytical Psychology, vol. 4. London: Society of Analytical Psychology, 1978.

Grimm Brothers. *The Complete Grimm's Fairy Tales.* London: Routledge and Kegan Paul, 1975.

Hillman, James. *Suicide and the Soul.* 2nd ed. Dallas: Spring Publications, 1976.

_____. *Archetypal Psychology. A Brief Account.* Dallas: Spring, 1983.

Holtved, E. "Eskimo Shamanism." In C.-M. Edsman, *Studies in Shamanism.* Stockholm: Almquist and Wiksell, 1967.

Jung, C.G. *The Collected Works* (Bollingen Series XX), 20 vols. Trans. R.F.C. Hull. Ed. H. Read, M. Fordham, G. Adler, Wm. McGuire. Princeton: Princeton University Press, 1953-1979.

_____. *Letters* (Bollingen Series XCV). 2 vols. Trans. R.F.C. Hull. Ed. G. Adler, A. Jaffé. Princeton: Princeton University Press, 1973.

_____. *Memories, Dreams, Reflections.* Ed. Aniela Jaffé. New York: Random House, 1963.

Jung, Emma, and von Franz, Marie-Louise. *The Grail Legend.* 2nd ed. Trans. Andrea Dykes. Boston: Sigo Press, 1986.

McGinnis, Alan Loy. *The Friendship Factor: How To Get Closer to the People You Care For.* Minneapolis: Augsburg Publishing House, 1979.

Moon, Sheila. *A Magic Dwells: A Poetic and Psychological Study of the Navaho Emergence Myth.* Middletown, CT: Wesleyan University Press, 1970.

Moore, S.F., and Myerhoff, B., eds. *Secular Rituals.* Amsterdam: Gorcum, 1977.

Neumann, Erich. *The Child.* Trans. R. Manheim. New York: Harper, 1976.

Otto, Rudolf. *The Idea of the Holy: An Inquiry into the Non-Rational Factor in the Idea of the Divine and Its Relation to the Rational.* London: Oxford University Press, 1950.

Perera, Sylvia Brinton. *Descent to the Goddess: A Way of Initiation for Women.* Toronto: Inner City Books, 1981.

Perry, John W. *The Far Side of Madness.* Englewood Cliffs, NJ: Prentice Hall, 1974.

Phelps, Ethel J. *The Maid of the North and Other Folktale Heroines.* New York: Holt, Rinehart and Winston, 1981.

Rappaport, R. "Ritual Sanctity and Cybernetics." *American Anthropologist,* 1: 59-76 (1973).

Rilke, Rainer Maria. *Briefe* [Letters]. Bern: Insel Verlag, 1953.

Rupp, Ph. "Die Verzweiflung des Analytikers: Ein Versuch ihrer Darstellung und Erklärung" [The Analyst's Despair: A Descriptive and Explanatory Essay]. Inaugural dissertation, Universität Innsbruck, 1972.

Storm, Hyemeyohsts. *Seven Arrows.* New York: Ballantine Books, 1973.

_____. *Song of Heyoehkah.* New York: Ballantine Books, 1981.

Ulanov, Ann. "The Witch Archetype." In *Quadrant,* vol. 10, no. 1 (1977).

Young-Eisendrath, Polly. *Hags and Heroes: A Feminist Approach to Jungian Psychotherapy with Couples.* Toronto: Inner City Books, 1984.

Turner, Victor. *The Ritual Process: Structure and Antistructure.* Chicago: Aldine, 1969.

van Gennep, Arnold. *The Rites of Passage.* London: Routledge and Kegan Paul, 1960.

Winnicott, D.W. *Playing and Reality.* London: Tavistock, 1971.

Ziegler, A.J. *Morbismus, von der Besten aller Gesundheiten* [Morbidism, the Best of Health]. Zürich: Schweizer Spiegel Verlag, 1979.

Index

By Edward F. Edinger

TRANSFORMATION OF THE GOD-IMAGE
An Elucidation of Jung's *Answer to Job*
Edited with a Foreword by Lawrence W. Jaffe
ISBN 0-919123-55-4. (1992) 144pp. *Sewn* $16

From the Foreword:
The special status of *Answer to Job* as the most complete statement of
Jung's essential message has long been acknowledged by Jungians, who
have discussed it in countless seminars and conferences since its publication in 1952.

What has sparked all this interest is that the central theme of *Answer to
Job*—the transformation of God through human consciousness—is the
central theme, too, of Jungian psychology. Not long before his death Jung
himself affirmed its importance, remarking that he would like to rewrite all
his books except *Answer to Job,* which he would leave just as it stands.

Answer to Job contains the kernel, the essence, of the Jungian myth,
and Edinger's singular study of it, at once erudite and down-to-earth,
thoughtful and heartfelt, evokes that essence with unequaled clarity and
power.

Studies in Jungian Psychology
by Jungian Analysts

Quality Paperbacks

Prices and payment in $US (except in Canada, $Cdn)

1. The Secret Raven: Conflict and Transformation
Daryl Sharp (Toronto). ISBN 0-919123-00-7. 128 pp. $16

2. The Psychological Meaning of Redemption Motifs in Fairy Tales
Marie-Louise von Franz (Zürich). ISBN 0-919123-01-5. 128 pp. $16

3. On Divination and Synchronicity: The Psychology of Meaningful Chance
Marie-Louise von Franz (Zürich). ISBN 0-919123-02-3. 128 pp. $16

4. The Owl Was a Baker's Daughter: Obesity, Anorexia and the Repressed Feminine Marion Woodman (Toronto). ISBN 0-919123-03-1. 144 pp. $16

5. Alchemy: An Introduction to the Symbolism and the Psychology
Marie-Louise von Franz (Zürich). ISBN 0-919123-04-X. 288 pp. $20

6. Descent to the Goddess: A Way of Initiation for Women
Sylvia Brinton Perera (New York). ISBN 0-919123-05-8. 112 pp. $16

7. The Psyche as Sacrament: A Comparative Study of Jung and Paul Tillich
John P. Dourley (Ottawa). ISBN 0-919123-06-6. 128 pp. $16

8. Border Crossings: Carlos Castaneda's Path of Knowledge
Donald Lee Williams (Boulder). ISBN 0-919123-07-4. 160 pp. $16

9. Narcissism and Character Transformation: The Psychology of Narcissistic Character Disorders
Nathan Schwartz-Salant (New York). ISBN 0-919123-08-2. 192 pp. $18

11. Alcoholism and Women: The Background and the Psychology
Jan Bauer (Montreal). ISBN 0-919123-10-4. 144 pp. $16

12. Addiction to Perfection: The Still Unravished Bride
Marion Woodman (Toronto). ISBN 0-919123-11-2. 208 pp. $18pb/$25hc

13. Jungian Dream Interpretation: A Handbook of Theory and Practice
James A. Hall, M.D. (Dallas). ISBN 0-919123-12-0. 128 pp. $16

14. The Creation of Consciousness: Jung's Myth for Modern Man
Edward F. Edinger (Los Angeles). ISBN 0-919123-13-9. 128 pp. $16

15. The Analytic Encounter: Transference and Human Relationship
Mario Jacoby (Zürich). ISBN 0-919123-14-7. 128 pp. $16

16. Change of Life: Dreams and the Menopause
Ann Mankowitz (Ireland). ISBN 0-919123-15-5. 128 pp. $16

17. The Illness That We Are: A Jungian Critique of Christianity
John P. Dourley (Ottawa). ISBN 0-919123-16-3. 128 pp. $16

18. Hags and Heroes: A Feminist Approach to Jungian Psychotherapy with Couples Polly Young-Eisendrath (Philadelphia). ISBN 0-919123-17-1. 192 pp. $18

19. Cultural Attitudes in Psychological Perspective
Joseph L. Henderson, M.D. (San Francisco). ISBN 0-919123-18-X. 128 pp. $16

20. The Vertical Labyrinth: Individuation in Jungian Psychology
Aldo Carotenuto (Rome). ISBN 0-919123-19-8. 144 pp. $16

21. The Pregnant Virgin: A Process of Psychological Transformation
Marion Woodman (Toronto). ISBN 0-919123-20-1. 208 pp. $18pb/$25hc

70. Psyche in Scripture: The Idea of the Chosen One and Other Essays
Rivkah Schärf Kluger (Israel). ISBN 0-919123-71-6. 128 pp. $16

71. The Aion Lectures: Exploring the Self in C.G. Jung's *Aion*
Edward F. Edinger (Los Angeles). ISBN 0-919123-72-4. 208 pp. $18

72. Living Jung: The Good and the Better
Daryl Sharp (Toronto). ISBN 0-919123-73-2. 128 pp. $16

73. Swamplands of the Soul: New Life in Dismal Places
James Hollis (Houston). ISBN 0-919123-74-0. 160 pp. $16

74. Food and Transformation: Imagery and Symbolism of Eating
Eve Jackson (London). ISBN 0-919123-75-9. 128 pp. $16

75. Archetypes & Strange Attractors: The Chaotic World of Symbols
John R. Van Eenwyk (Olympia, WA). ISBN 0-919123-76-7. 192 pp. $18

76. Archetypal Patterns in Fairy Tales
Marie-Louise von Franz (Zurich). ISBN 0-919123-77-5. 192 pp. $18

77. C.G. Jung: His Myth in Our Time
Marie-Louise von Franz (Zurich). ISBN 0-919123-78-3. 368 pp. $25

78. Divine Tempest: The Hurricane As a Psychic Phenomenon
David E. Schoen (New Orleans). ISBN 0-919123-79-1. 128 pp. $16

79. The Eden Project: In Search of the Magical Other
James Hollis (Houston). ISBN 0-919123-80-5. 160 pp. $16

80. Jungian Psychology Unplugged: My Life As an Elephant
Daryl Sharp (Toronto). ISBN 0-919123-81-3. 160 pp. $16

82. Now or Neverland: Peter Pan and the Myth of Eternal Youth
Ann Yeoman (Toronto). ISBN 0-919123-83-X. 192 pp. $18

83. The Cat: A Tale of Feminine Redemption
Marie-Louise von Franz (Zurich). ISBN 0-919123-84-8. 160 pp. $16

84. Celebrating Soul: Preparing for the New Religion
Lawrence W. Jaffe (Berkeley, CA). ISBN 0-919123-85-6. 128 pp. $16

85. The Psyche in Antiquity, Book 1: Early Greek Philosophy
Edward F. Edinger (Los Angeles). ISBN 0-919123-86-4. 128 pp. $16

86. The Psyche in Antiquity, Book 2: Gnosticism and Early Christianity
Edward F. Edinger (Los Angeles). ISBN 0-919123-87-2. 160 pp. $16

87. The Problem of the Puer Aeternus
Marie-Louise von Franz (Zurich). ISBN 0-919123-88-0. 288 pp. $20

88. The Inner Journey: Lectures and Essays on Jungian Psychology
Barbara Hannah (Zurich). ISBN 0-919123-89-9. 160 pp. $16

89. Aurora Consurgens: A Document Attributed to Thomas Aquinas
Commentary by Marie-Louise von Franz (Zurich). ISBN 0-919123-90-2. 576 pp. $36

90. Ego and Self: The Old Testament Prophets
Edward F. Edinger (Zurich). ISBN 0-919123-91-0. 160 pp. $16

Discounts: any 3-5 books, 10%; 6-9 books, 20%; 10 or more, 25%
Add Postage/Handling: 1-2 books, $3; 3-4 books, $5; 5-9 books, $10; 10 or more, free

Credit cards: Contact BookWorld toll-free: 1-800-444-2524, or Fax 1-800-777-2525

Free Catalogue and **Jung at Heart** newsletter:

INNER CITY BOOKS, Box 1271, Station Q, Toronto, ON M4T 2P4, Canada
Tel. 416-927-0355 / Fax: 416-924-1814 / E-mail: icb@inforamp.net